Birds of Northeast Texas

NUMBER THIRTY-TWO
W. L. Moody, Jr., Natural History Series

Birds of Northeast Texas

MATT WHITE

Foreword by Greg W. Lasley

TEXAS A&M UNIVERSITY PRESS   COLLEGE STATION

First edition

The paper used in this book
meets the minimum requirements
of the American National Standard
for Permanence of Paper for Printed
Library Materials, z39.48-1984.
Binding materials have been
chosen for durability.

Library of Congress Cataloging-in-Publication Data

White, Matt, 1967–
Birds of Northeast Texas / Matt White ; foreword by
Greg W. Lasley.—1st ed.
p. cm.—(W.L. Moody, Jr., natural history series ; no. 32)
Includes bibliographical references (p.) and index.
ISBN 1-58544-192-9 (cloth : alk. paper)—
ISBN 1-58544-193-7 (pbk. : alk. paper)
1. Birds—Texas—Indentification. I. Title. II. Series.
QL684.T4W48 2002
598'.09764'2—dc21 2001006544

CONTENTS

List of Illustrations VII

Foreword by Greg W. Lasley IX

Acknowledgments XI

Introduction 3

1. Geography of the Region 8

2. Birdwatching Areas 13

3. Species Accounts 26

    Definition of Terms 26

    Species Occurring in Northeast Texas 27

    Hypothetical Species 114

    Extirpated Species 117

    Introduced Species 119

Bibliography 121

Index 123

ILLUSTRATIONS

Photos follow page 28

1. Pied-billed Grebe
2. Horned Grebes
3. American White Pelicans
4. Black-crowned Night-Heron
5. Adult Glossy Ibis and White-faced Ibis
6. Turkey Vultures
7. Snow Geese and Greater White-fronted Geese
8. Black Scoters
9. Red-tailed Hawk
10. Semipalmated Plover
11. American Avocets
12. Ruddy Turnstone
13. Dunlin
14. Common Snipe
15. Black-headed Gull
16. Bonaparte's Gulls
17. Common Tern
18. Black Tern
19. Black Skimmer
20. Common Ground-Dove
21. Scissor-tailed Flycatchers
22. White-breasted Nuthatches
23. Rock Wren
24. Bewick's Wren

25. American Pipit
26. Le Conte's Sparrow
27. Eastern Bluebird
28. Lapland Longspur
29. Smith's Longspur
30. Yellow-headed Blackbirds

FOREWORD

The long-awaited publication of Harry C. Oberholser's seminal *The Bird Life of Texas* in 1974 brought both amateur and professional students of Texas ornithology a complete and detailed analysis of the birds in this state. As the popularity of birdwatching grew, a need arose for more regional information on various parts of the state, and recent years have seen publication of a host of books expanding upon Oberholser's work in various ways. There are now books available giving an accurate picture of the status and distribution of birds from north-central Texas, the central coast, the Edwards Plateau, the Trans-Pecos, and the Panhandle. Authors are currently working on similar books for the Lower Rio Grande Valley and the upper Texas coast. Together, such works provide uniquely detailed views of the bird life in each of these areas, documenting occurrences more thoroughly than is possible in a general book about the state as a whole.

Now Matt White has provided us with a book on the birds of Northeast Texas. In *Birds of Northeast Texas* he offers summaries of the status of the 390 species that have been reliably recorded from that region. It might be considered an overlooked area for birdwatchers in Texas; indeed, it is a marvelous region full of surprises for the birder.

Northeast Texas has a large number of reservoirs, several of which have become almost legend among serious Texas birders in the past decade. Places like Lake Tawakoni, Lake O' the Pines, Wright Patman Reservoir, and others have become destinations for birders seeking rare winter loons and grebes, waterfowl, and gulls. The grasslands in the region are some of the best in the state for seeing longspurs and sparrows, while the woodlands, marshes, and swamplands attract a wide variety of breeding warblers, vireos, woodpeckers, and other groups of birds. Birders from across the state are now beginning to discover the many gems of wildlife habitat that Northeast Texas offers. Matt's book should increase this awareness and provide the bird student with baseline data concerning the species that occur there.

Matt White grew up in Northeast Texas, and anyone who has spent time with him can easily feel his love for the area. He has tramped across much of this region and has developed a thoroughgoing competence with and understanding of the birds that live here. His perceptions and analyses of the region's bird life are accurate, and he has developed into one of the most knowledgeable field observers in Texas. Matt sheds light on Northeast Texas bird populations that has been lacking in the past, and he offers the birdwatcher information on the area that has not been available before.

I have been fortunate enough to spend some time in Northeast Texas with Matt, who has taught me a great deal about this region of the state. He is one of those individuals who is always careful to document his rarity records with written details and often photographs. Through his efforts, many species previously considered hypothetical in Northeast Texas have now been fully documented as members of the avifauna of that area. As Matt notes in his introduction, this book is the first attempt to delineate the status and distribution of the birds in the area and should be considered an initial effort. As our knowledge increases and the number of birders visiting the area continues to grow, no doubt further important discoveries await us.

Northeast Texas has a small but knowledgeable and very dedicated group of serious birders whose sightings constitute a key component of the records cited in this book. I hope members of this group will continue their efforts and attract new birdwatchers into the fold so that the database can continue to grow. Many new avian experiences await us all in Northeast Texas. I'll see you there!

Greg W. Lasley

ACKNOWLEDGMENTS

This book would not have been possible without the skill, determination and input of dozens of people who have faithfully reported their sightings over the years—some of whom are no longer with us. I especially thank the members of the Northeast Texas Field Ornithologists, who have helped reveal the fascinating birdlife of this region.

Peter Barnes and Jim Ingold read the entire manuscript and made numerous helpful suggestions. Their assistance is greatly appreciated. Special thanks are also due to Greg Lasley, who has gone out of his way to be helpful—his generosity and kindness are exemplary. I am also grateful to Charles Mills, who responded to numerous requests for information. Delbert Tarter provided insightful glimpses into the distribution and habitat of Bell's Vireo a half century ago. Jim Conrad, archivist at Gee Library, Texas A&M University–Commerce, provided historical material that was especially valuable. Dorothy Metzler kindly provided material that was invaluable. David Hurt provided valuable assistance and encouragement. I would also like to thank Shannon Davies for her support and belief in this book. Last, but certainly not least, I want to thank my parents and my wife and children for tolerating my constant birding. Without their support this book would not have been possible.

Birds of Northeast Texas

Introduction

According to recent surveys, birdwatching is one of the fastest growing hobbies in the United States. Several million people now enjoy watching birds in one way or another. Although most simply feed the birds that visit their backyards, many others travel hundreds or even thousands of miles each year looking for birds. That birdwatching continues to attract burgeoning numbers of new enthusiasts each year is evident in the dizzying array of new field guides that come out annually. In various ways, many of these new guides are aimed at helping people appreciate the wonders of the avian world by allowing them to identify the birds they see. For each species, most field guides have fairly accurate range maps that are helpful in allowing observers to find out if a certain kind of bird breeds, or spends the winter, in a particular area. However, it is often difficult to obtain additional information about the abundance of birds that regularly migrate through a particular region or about those that visit only rarely. Therefore books about the local status and distribution of birds are particularly important for people who want to learn more about the birds of their area.

The *Birds of Northeast Texas* is a guide to the 390 species that have been recorded reliably in Northeast Texas and is designed to accompany any of the excellent field guides that are on the market today. The brief species accounts explain each species' status, distribution, and period of occurrence in the region. Many accounts also include a short commentary about habitat preference, unusual records, or some other aspect that is interesting or unique about that particular species. Just as knowing what to look for is a crucial part of being a successful birdwatcher; knowing when and where to look are equally important and will add to your success at finding birds.

The species accounts are followed by a list of hypothetical species—a term for birds that remain poorly documented for the region—particularly old records with no details and recent ones that are very rare in the state or area. This category includes Texas Review Species (see later discussion) that for one reason or another have not been accepted. Although many of the hypothetical birds have probably occurred in Northeast Texas, more evidence is needed before they can be added to the list with confidence. Sadly, a few species no longer occur. These include birds that are now thought to be extinct, species for which numbers have declined in recent years, and birds with ranges that no longer include Northeast Texas. Finally, there is one introduced species that may or may not be established. However, just as it is beyond the scope of the field guides to provide detailed information about the birds of this or any other particular region, it is beyond the scope of this book to help readers identify all of the birds in Northeast Texas.

Many states and a growing number of regions within them now have similar guides to their birds. Harry C. Oberholser's monumental *The Bird Life of Texas,* published in 1974, remains one of the most thorough works about the birds of any state. Naturally, much has been learned since then, so in order to keep pace, the Texas Ornithological Society publishes its *Checklist of the Birds of Texas,* which is updated about every ten years—most recently in 1995. This small but useful publication is not intended to deliver the kind of extensive detail presented in *The Bird Life of Texas.* Instead, it updates our ever-changing understanding of the birds of this huge state in a timely manner. The concise accounts are designed to provide thumbnail sketches detailing the abundance and range of the more than six hundred species now recorded in the state. A few regions of Texas have similar guides, though until now Northeast Texas has been overlooked.

As it is delineated in this book, Northeast Texas includes twenty-two counties in the northeastern corner of the state (see map under Birdwatching Areas). The region is bounded to the north by the Red River and by Fannin, Hunt, and Van Zandt counties to the west. The eastern boundary is formed by the state border with Arkansas and Louisiana and includes a short stretch of the Sabine River. The southern limits are Panola, Rusk, Smith, and Van Zandt counties.

This region is a popular destination for many people seeking various types of outdoor recreation, chiefly fishing, boating, hunting, hiking, and camping. Birdwatchers have recently discovered the potential of the region and the number of people who visit for this purpose has grown considerably. Many birdwatchers reside in the region's urban centers, including Texarkana, Paris, Greenville, Tyler, Longview, Mount Pleasant, and Marshall, though a growing number travel from nearby Dallas and Fort Worth as well as from other states and several foreign countries.

Northeast Texas has one of the largest concentrations of artificial reservoirs in Texas. Some of the larger ones—such as Lake Fork Reservoir, Lake Tawakoni, and Lake Bob Sandlin—attract thousands of visitors annually, mainly for fishing. However, these lakes are also popular among birdwatchers, and their close scrutiny in recent years has profoundly altered our understanding of the bird life of the region and the state as a whole. These large inland bodies of water serve as magnets for birds, attracting a range of species that are very rare in the state. In the past five years alone, some of the stellar rarities that have been seen here are Yellow-billed Loon, Harlequin Duck, Barrow's Goldeneye, Long-tailed Jaeger, and Roseate Tern. A number of species now occur more or less regularly, including Red-throated and Pacific loons, all three species of scoters, Long-tailed Duck, Black-legged Kittiwake, and Sabine's Gull. Perhaps the region's most sought-after bird is the Smith's Longspur—a small, nondescript member of the sparrow clan that spends a few weeks each winter hiding in our cattle pastures. Since the species was discovered there some years ago, thousands of birders have trekked to Lake Tawakoni, possibly the best place in all of Texas to see them.

The birds of Northeast Texas were first studied in the late nineteenth century and the early twentieth century, but only a handful of people published their findings. In the last fifty years or so, the number of people who have sought to contribute to our understanding of the birds of this region has grown slowly, and interest has largely been confined to a few selected areas. Much of this early work was included (although often without details) in Oberholser's *The Bird Life of Texas.* Over the last fifty years, a few people have contributed their sightings for publication in *Audubon Field Notes,* which later became *American Birds* and which until recently was a publication of the National Audubon Society that sought to provide seasonal details four times a year about bird sightings from all over North America. The American Birding Association publishes this quarterly magazine today under the name *North American Birds.* This periodical continues to publish the sighting of individuals in Northeast Texas and is an important source of information.

There has never been a thorough treatment of the region's avifauna, though Warren Pulich's *Birds of North Central Texas,* published in 1988, included four of the western counties treated here. Since 1990 the most active group has been the Northeast Texas Field Ornithologists (NETFO), headquartered in Longview. Their monthly publication, the *NETFO Newsletter,* contains monthly sightings from throughout the region and is a valuable source of current information about the birds in this region. A number of other people have birded various parts the region for years, and their contributions should not be understated.

Additional fieldwork is needed to add missing pieces to the puzzle, even in a relatively heavily populated region like Northeast Texas. But this is what makes birdwatching so much fun. As long as there are places that still need exploring, and birds that remain unfound, birdwatchers will continue to search for them—in turn adding more pieces to the puzzle. *Birds of Northeast Texas* is the first attempt to put the various pieces of the puzzle together for this region. Like any work of this nature, it must be seen as an initial effort, the publication of which will spur others to add to our knowledge in the future, I hope. The taxonomy in the book follows the seventh edition of the American Ornithologists' Union *Check-list of North American Birds,* published in 1998, as currently supplemented.

A word should also be said about the Texas Bird Records Committee (TBRC). Since 1975 the members of this committee of the Texas Ornithological Society have collected and archived for future reference all documentation submitted for rare and unusual species that have occurred in the state. Documentation may be in the form of photographs, field drawings, detailed notes, or audio or video recordings. The all-volunteer TBRC maintains a list of Review Species, the rarest of the rare in the state, for which documentation is always requested. This list, many photographs, and the forms for documenting rarities can be viewed on or downloaded from the attractive website that the TBRC maintains on the Internet (http://members.tripod.com/~tbrc/). The decisions of the committee are published annually, both on the website and in the *Bulletin of the Texas Ornithological Society.* The TBRC also collects photographs of rare and unusual birds; these photos are archived in the Texas Photo Records File (TPRF) housed at Texas A&M University.

The importance of this task cannot be stated too strongly. There are many old reports of rare birds in Northeast Texas that lack any form of documentation, making it difficult to judge their validity today. A good example is an old report of a Snowy Owl from the 1920s near Commerce. Today this would be an incredible record as this arctic owl seldom visits the state. By submitting details for rare birds that you observe, you will be helping to preserve for future generations the ornithological history of the state and the region. A number of these Review Species have occurred in Northeast Texas, and the accounts for those species in this book include the TBRC number that is assigned to each record and, if available, the TPRF number. If you observe any of these species while in the region (or the state), please contact the secretary of the committee via the TBRC website.

CHAPTER I

Geography of the Region

Although the scenery of Northeast Texas may look homogeneous to visitors driving along Interstate 30 from Dallas to Texarkana, or along I-20 from Dallas to Longview, the region actually encompasses a wider diversity of habitat than many realize. From the White Rock Escarpment (with its affinity to the Texas Hill Country) to the Pineywoods and the swamps of Caddo Lake (with their affinity to the Louisiana swamps and bayous), the region lies strategically in a transition zone between the habitat types centered to the east and west. Most people traveling east on either of these two modern thoroughfares may not notice as the Blackland Prairie gives way to Post Oak Savannah, but even the casual observer usually notices the tall pine trees of the Pineywoods. The contrast between the east and the west within the region is quite dramatic and is tied to a number of factors, such as annual rainfall and composition. The western counties of Northeast Texas receive an average of thirty-six inches of rainfall a year, while those on the extreme eastern edge receive an average of forty-five inches or more. The dark, fertile clay soils in the west are replaced by deep sandy loam in the east.

White Rock Escarpment

The White Rock Escarpment is a microhabitat of the Blackland Prairie in portions of northern Hunt County as well as parts of

Fannin, Lamar, and Red River counties. The dark clay topsoil is shallow (often no more than eighteen inches deep) and rests upon a thick layer of fragmented and easily broken white limestone, known locally as chalk or white rock. The vegetation is similar to that of the Balcones Escarpment in the Texas Hill Country. Several trees and flowers that are found in abundance here are uncommon or absent elsewhere in Northeast Texas, such as chinquapin oak and Texas red oak. A good place to view this habitat is at Bonham State Park in Fannin County.

Blackland Prairie

The western third of Northeast Texas lies within the physiographic region known as the Blackland Prairie. Once a vast sea of tall grasses, today the Blackland Prairie is largely an agricultural and developed region that stretches in a narrow band from Austin in Central Texas to Sherman and Clarksville near the Red River. The soils consist of eroded limestone and dark organic matter, hence the name. Early pioneers were impressed by the fertility of this soil for growing crops, and today less than one tenth of 1 percent of virgin grasslands remain intact. Most of the few small patches that have never met the plow were preserved as hay meadows and are now valuable "islands" of prairie plants.

There are more trees today on these prairies than there were when the first European settlers arrived a century and a half ago. Fire was once a critical component in the maintenance of this ecosystem. Fires were apparently ignited by Indians as well as by natural causes, such as lightning, and helped prevent woody vegetation from becoming established. Fire suppression in recent years has allowed trees to invade into the region. As recently as the 1850s, bison were still roaming these grasslands and helping to maintain the prairie by grazing young trees before they became tall enough to become established. Years ago trees were confined mostly along creeks and rivers, but today they are found widely in abandoned fields that are no longer grazed or plowed and along fences. The most common trees include cedar elm, sugar hackberry, bois d' arc, eastern red cedar, honey locust, and persimmon. Cottonwood, pecan, hickory, and box elder are especially common along the creek and river bottoms. Less common are bur oak, soapberry, and Eve's necklace. Rough-leaf dogwood and redbud are common, and poison ivy, green briar, and dewberry are abundant understory forbs. On the prairies the most common grasses and wildflowers include Indiangrass, little bluestem, big bluestem, Maxmillian sunflower, purple coneflower, Indian blanket and Indian paintbrush. Today cattle grazing and row crops such as cotton and sorghum are widespread.

The Blackland Prairie supports the lowest number of breeding birds in the region. The most common breeding birds in the grasslands are probably Dickcissels, Common Grackles, and Brown-headed Cowbirds. Eastern Meadowlarks and Grasshopper Sparrows are found in some old fields and lightly grazed pastures. Horned Larks and Lark Sparrows are common in plowed fields, as are Killdeer. Northern Mockingbirds, Scissor-tailed Flycatchers, and Western Kingbirds are found where trees or shrubs are present, also favoring telephone poles. The scrubby areas harbor Painted Buntings and Blue Grosbeaks. In the wooded parts of the region, Carolina Chickadees, Tufted Titmice, Northern Cardinals, and Carolina Wrens are most common, but even in these wooded areas, the breeding bird diversity is quite low.

In winter and during migration, this area is home to a more diverse array of birds. The plowed fields host hordes of Lapland Longspurs and Horned Larks. American Kestrels and Loggerhead Shrikes hunt for small prey from the telephone wires, and Red-tailed Hawks and Northern Harriers course the fields. The brushy fences and scrubby woods are home to large numbers of sparrows. Thousands of ducks and geese use this region as a migratory corridor, and increasingly, many winter in the large winter wheat fields.

Post Oak Savannah

To the east of the Blackland Prairie and north along the Red River lies the Post Oak Savannah, a region of dry sandy soil supporting a mix of upland post oak woodlands and scattered grasslands. Much of the central portion of Northeast Texas lies within this habitat, which is actually a transitional area, or ecotone, between the deep woodlands of East Texas and the open grasslands of the west. Many of the same tree species that occur on the prairies occur in the post oak savannah as well, though the dominant trees here are oaks—post, blackjack, water, willow, red, and black oaks. The river and creek bottoms are much wetter than other sections of the Post Oak Savannah and support a wider variety of flora and fauna. In many places large areas of trees have been cleared, making parts of this region look almost indistinguishable from the Blackland Prairie. Cattle ranches, dairy farms, and hay meadows are common throughout this area.

Key breeding birds include Eastern Bluebird, White-breasted Nuthatch, Summer Tanager, Eastern Kingbird, Black-and-white Warbler, Carolina Wren, Tufted Titmouse, Carolina Chickadee, and Yellow-billed Cuckoo. Cooper Lake State Park, Lake Tawakoni, and Purtis Creek State Park are all good examples of this habitat.

Pineywoods

The East Texas Pineywoods make up the remainder of Northeast Texas. This region was once densely wooded with a mix of very tall pines and oaks. As in the Blackland Prairie, here too less than one tenth of 1 percent of the original habitat—in this case virgin forest—remains intact. Most forests were cut for timber and to clear the land for agriculture or development. The native mix of trees in this region was a great deal richer than the range of tree species mainly seen today. Pines are usually replanted exclusively because they grow faster. However, these pine plantations support far fewer breeding birds than the native mix of pines and oaks. This part of Northeast Texas still fosters the greatest diversity of breeding birds in the region, especially in the low-lying and frequently flooded creek and river bottoms. These seasonal wetlands provide critical habitat.

Most of the same trees that occur in the Post Oak Savannah and Blackland Prairie grow here, though loblolly and shortleaf pines are much more evident. Flowering dogwood and sweetgum are more common here than elsewhere. Thirteen species of warblers, four vireos, and dozens of other kinds of songbirds breed. The state parks at Atlanta, Lake Bob Sandlin, Martin Creek Lake, and Caddo Lake are typical of this habitat.

Red River Corridor

Today little remains of the vast bottomland hardwood forest that once covered the wide Red River Valley. Ten miles wide or more in some places, this floodplain forest was actually a seasonal wetland and supported a diverse array of wildlife before it was mostly cleared and drained for hay meadows and cattle pastures. The high bluffs on the south side of the valley are covered with deep sandy soil and allow a number of plants typical of the woodlands of eastern Texas to extend farther westward than elsewhere. Good places to see this habitat are Sander's Cove at Pat Mayse Lake in Lamar County and at the Caddo National Grasslands in Fannin County.

CHAPTER 2

Birdwatching Areas

Northeast Texas has ten state parks offering public property for birdwatching. They encompass a range of habitats, although a disproportionate number are in the Pineywoods. Most are situated on area lakes and provide easy public viewing access to the water (see map).

There are also a few U.S. Army Corps of Engineers parks as well as other sites of interest that are not part of the excellent Texas park system. In addition there are a handful of preserves owned by the Nature Conservancy that protect some of the finest natural habitat in Northeast Texas, including three native prairies and a true old growth forest. Of course, these are certainly not the only places in the region that afford enjoyable birdwatching. Many back roads, public cemeteries, city parks, and similar areas are great places for birding and offer a chance for exploration. All you need are a map, binoculars, and willingness to explore. Several of these sites are featured in the second edition of Edward Kutac's *Birder's Guide to Texas* and in Roland Wauer's and Mark Elwonger's *Birding Texas.*

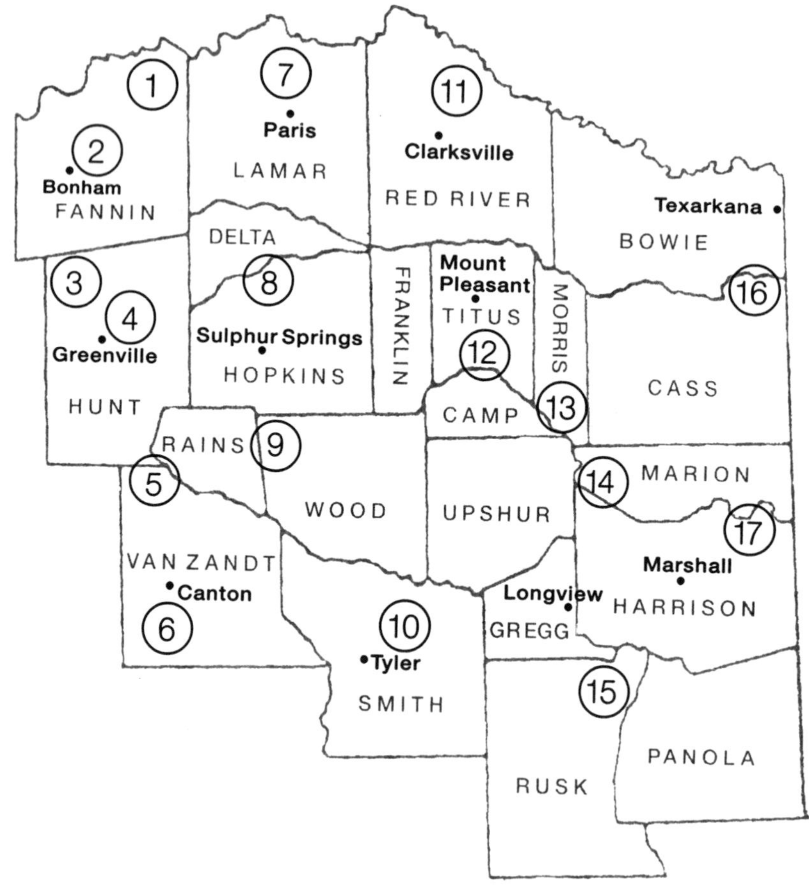

BIRDING LOCATIONS IN NORTHEAST TEXAS KEYED TO MAP

1. Caddo National Grasslands
2. Bonham State Park
3. Clymer Meadow Native Prairie
4. Greenville City Lakes
5. Lake Tawakoni
6. Purtis Creek State Park
7. Pat Mayse Lake
8. Cooper Lake
9. Lake Fork
10. Tyler State Park/Camp Tyler
11. Lennox Woods Old Growth Forest
12. Lake Cypress Springs/Lake Monticello/Lake Bob Sandlin/Lake Bob Sandlin State Park
13. Daingerfield State Park
14. Lake O' the Pines
15. Martin Creek Lake State Park
16. Wright Patman Reservoir/Atlanta State Park
17. Caddo Lake/Caddo Lake State Park

State Parks and Reservoirs

ATLANTA STATE PARK

(At Wright Patman Reservoir)
RR 1, Box 116
Atlanta, Texas 75551
(903) 796-6476

This large reservoir is located on the Sulphur River in the extreme northeastern corner of the state and may be one of the best underbirded lakes in the state. Pine Warblers, Brown-headed Nuthatches, and Chipping Sparrows breed within the state park, as do an array of eastern woodland species such as Summer Tanagers, White-breasted Nuthatches, and Black-and-white Warblers. In winter the bluestem fields harbor a fairly large number of Le Conte's Sparrows and possibly a few Henslow's Sparrows as well.

The real attraction of Wright Patman for birdwatchers, though, is the open water of the lake, where observers have recently discovered an unusual number of rarities, particularly in winter. The open water of the lake should be scanned for waterfowl, especially Surf and White-winged scoters and Long-tailed Ducks. If water is being discharged through the floodgates under the dam (outside the park), hundreds of Bonaparte's Gulls and Forster's Terns often feed over the discharge channel, occasionally attracting rarities such as Black-headed or Little gulls or Black-legged Kittiwakes.

BONHAM STATE PARK

RR 1, Box 337
Bonham, Texas 75418
(903) 679-3351

Situated atop a high ridge in the microhabitat known as the White Rock Escarpment, Bonham State Park protects a small piece of this unique habitat. Mature cedar brakes mixed with oaks on the steep hills are reminiscent of the Hill Country and seem out of place in Northeast Texas. The park is mainly a recreational park—

a swimming beach on a small lake and a campground are the biggest attractions for the general public. Although little birding has been done here, it is a place ripe with potential. A relict of habitat that was once more widespread, a few of the hilly slopes are dotted with much younger cedar thickets and may once have supported a small Black-capped Vireo population. The park should prove an attractive place to find winter sparrows as the surrounding lands have largely been cleared for cattle or cotton farming.

The habitat varies from riparian woodlands to dry ridges covered with mature and dense eastern red cedars, Texas red oak, and chinquapin oak. Carolina buckthorn, aromatic sumac, and rattan vine grow in the thin topsoil on the rocky slopes. Bonham State Park was built as a Civilian Conservation Corps campground in the 1930s, and the park's historic stone buildings date to that era.

CADDO LAKE STATE PARK

RR 2, Box 14
Karnack, Texas 75661
(903) 679-1112

The only natural lake in Texas, Caddo Lake is a vast swampy labyrinth full of tall cypress trees laden with Spanish moss. Looking more like a Louisiana bayou than an inland Texas lake, this is a primitive place full of interesting scenery and history. The birds here, too, are worth a visit. During spring and summer you may be overwhelmed by the number of Northern Parulas and Prothonotary Warblers. A number of other warbler species breed in the park or its vicinity, including Swainson's, Prairie, Pine, Yellow-throated, Black-and-white, and Kentucky Warblers and Louisiana Waterthrush. Listen also for the flutelike song of the Wood Thrush or the staccato "wake-up" calls of the sluggish Acadian Flycatchers in spring and summer. All the common birds of the eastern forests are found as well. Purple Gallinules have been seen in the more vegetated parts of the lake, so keep your eyes open to that possibility also. Pileated Woodpeckers are found year-round and are often easy to see.

COOPER LAKE STATE PARK

South Sulphur Unit
RR 1, Box 231-A5
Cooper, Texas 75432

Doctor's Creek Unit
RR 3, Box 741
Sulphur Springs, Texas 75482

Completed in 1991, Cooper Lake on the South Sulphur River is the region's newest lake. It is located where the Blackland Prairie meets the Post Oak Savannah and is an appealing area for birdwatching because of its habitat diversity. One of the most beautiful sections consists of cedar thickets in the old fields and pastures below the dam, designated as a Watchable Wildlife area. Currently parking facilities are limited, and access via the long road over the dam is forbidden by the U.S. Army Corps of Engineers, who built it and maintain it. Viewing access to the lake from this road is also off-limits; regulations against stopping, walking, or standing on the dam are rigidly enforced.

Cooper Lake State Park is divided into two separate units, each with slightly different habitats. The South Sulphur Unit located at the southern end of Cooper Lake takes in more than twenty-three hundred acres of hilly Post Oak Savannah. This unit is much more forested than the other and contains more breeding species, including Black-and-white and Kentucky Warblers, White-breasted Nuthatches, and Summer Tanagers. A few Acadian Flycatchers breed, as do Hairy Woodpeckers. Field Sparrows trill in summer from the old fields, where in winter American Woodcock can sometimes be found. Both Eastern and Spotted Towhees are found in roughly equal numbers.

The Doctor's Creek Unit is much smaller—only 715 acres in size—and is more open and brushy. Aside from the usual cardinals and chickadees, few species breed here. This area is much better for winter sparrows, such as Harris's Sparrows, which seem to avoid heavily wooded habitats in favor of brushy and weedy fields. They are often found in flocks of White-crowned and White-throated sparrows in dense brush or weedy fields. A few Bewick's Wrens from the declining eastern populations remain in the park from October through February. This is often a good place from which to view the open water of the lake, where a number of rarities have been found in recent years.

DAINGERFIELD STATE PARK

Rt. 3, Box 283-B
Daingerfield, Texas 75638
(903) 645-2921

Located outside the East Texas town of Daingerfield, this small state park is nestled around a pretty little lake. The habitat consists of dense pine and hardwood forests. A large hill overlooking the lake is popular among local birders as a favorite place in fall to watch for migrating hawks. Following the passage of a cool front in September or October, a few hundred Broad-winged Hawks and lesser numbers of American Kestrels and Sharp-shinned and Cooper's hawks can be observed. Peregrine Falcons and Merlins have been seen as well. Also recorded from this prominent lookout, which affords a good view over the surrounding woods, are Wood Storks, Anhingas, and American White Pelicans migrating south.

Key breeding species are Pine Warblers and Brown-headed Nuthatches as well as most of the other woodland birds common in eastern Texas.

LAKE BOB SANDLIN STATE PARK

RR 5, Box 224
Pittsburg, Texas 75686
(903) 572-5531

The mix of pines, hardwoods, and bluestem fields makes Lake Bob Sandlin State Park an interesting place to visit, especially in spring when the dogwood and redbud trees are blooming, or in fall when the sweetgum trees and the red oaks are aflame. The birdlife is similar to that found elsewhere in East Texas, but several species are close to the western limit of their ranges here, such as Brown-headed Nuthatch and Pine Warbler. In winter the bluestem fields harbor Le Conte's Sparrows and probably Henslow's Sparrows as well.

Although just outside the state park, Lake Bob Sandlin is well known among local birders for a large open field, used as an emergency overflow for the lake, which lies just west of the dam. This area is maintained as a park by the nearby city of Mount Pleasant and is a great place to spend a day birding. The grass is kept short in winter, and Smith's and Chestnut-collared longspurs have been found on rare occasions. Western Meadowlarks sing in winter, and the cattail marsh near the dam harbors a few Sedge and Marsh wrens all winter. When the water level is low, the shore here is one of the best places in the Pineywoods of northeast Texas to find shorebirds. American Avocets are often seen, and Northeast Texas rarities such as Long-billed Curlew and Whimbrel have been recorded. During midwinter it is not hard to find a Bald Eagle perched in a dead tree. Greater Scaup are regular, and in recent years the Texas Review Species Red-necked Grebe and Black-legged Kittiwake have been seen.

Lake Bob Sandlin and nearby Lake Monticello and Lake Cypress Springs are popular fishing destinations, but the diversity of habitat makes this set of lakes a great birding destination as well.

LAKE TAWAKONI STATE PARK

c/o State Park Region 8
1638 Park Rd. 16
Tyler, Texas 75706-9132
(903) 598-2938

This new state park (yet to be opened for public use at the time of writing), lies beside Lake Tawakoni, one the prime birding destinations in Texas. Created in 1960 by a long earthen dam on the Sabine River, this large lake is a magnet for rare and unusual birds.

It is maintained by the Sabine River Authority, which openly welcomes birders by allowing access to the top of the dam (which is off-limits to the general public) on weekdays from 8:00 A.M. to 4:30 P.M. The list of rare birds seen from the dam is long and reads rather like a wish list for many visiting birders. Three species of loons, all three species of scoters, and a number of rare gulls, such as Black-headed, Glaucous, Thayer's, and Black-legged Kittiwake, have been recorded. Parasitic and Long-tailed jaegers have also been recorded, and in January 1995 a pair of Harlequin Ducks was observed near the spillway. The lake is the best place in Texas to find the unusual and elusive Smith's Longspurs, which winter by the dozen in the shortgrass fields beside the dam, along with an occasional Sprague's Pipit. Dallas County Audubon Society maintains a small sanctuary on a nearby cove, where Le Conte's and Henslow's sparrows are typically found in winter.

MARTIN CREEK LAKE STATE PARK

RR 2, Box 20
Tatum, Texas 75691
(903) 836-4336

As is typical of deep East Texas, Martin Creek State Park is dominated by tall pine trees and various hardwoods. For the last few years, several Tree Swallows have summered at Martin Lake and are nesting in old woodpecker holes in the dead trees in the water. This is a good place to find native sparrows in winter.

PURTIS CREEK STATE PARK

14225 FM 316
Eustace, Texas 75124
(903) 425-2332

Purtis Creek State Park south of Canton surrounds a small lake of some three hundred acres and is a great place to look for several eastern species at the western limit of their ranges, such as Acadian Flycatcher and Kentucky Warbler, and western species at the eastern limit of their ranges, such as Western Kingbird and Scissor-tailed Flycatcher. In late summer Wood Storks, Roseate Spoonbills, White Ibis, and other post-nesting wanderers from the south may occur. The small lake is popular with anglers, and only recently have birders started visiting.

TYLER STATE PARK

1638 Park Road 16
Tyler, Texas 75706-9132
(903) 597-5338

Tyler State Park is typical of the East Texas Pineywoods, with a mix of pines, hardwoods, and open fields. The birdlife is typical as well and includes breeding Black-and-white, Yellow-throated, and Pine warblers, Brown-headed Nuthatch, Summer Tanager, and Painted Bunting, to name just a few. In winter, common sparrows include Field, Chipping, Song, and White-throated sparrows. Look for Le Conte's and the rare Henslow's sparrows in the tall grassy fields.

Other Areas

CADDO NATIONAL GRASSLANDS

Located in Fannin County, the Caddo National Grasslands comprises several disjunct units. The main unit, near the small town of Telephone, is located on a bluff just south of the Red River bottoms and more closely resembles a national forest. Although the habitat consists of Post Oak Savannah, a reforestation project many years ago involved planting hundreds of loblolly and shortleaf pines that are now mature. These pines support a small but healthy disjunct population of Pine and Yellow-throated warblers. Recently American Goldfinches have been found singing here in summer, and they may be breeding. Field, Grasshopper, and Lark sparrows breed, as do Scissor-tailed Flycatchers and Eastern Kingbirds. There is a small population of breeding Broad-winged Hawks, alongside the usual Red-shouldered and Red-tailed hawks. A few Mississippi Kites likely breed as well. Fish Crows are present all summer and are probably breeding. A Christmas Bird Count here each winter usually tallies between ninety and a hundred species.

PAT MAYSE LAKE AND SANDERS COVE PARK

Located a few miles north of Paris on the Red River, Pat Mayse Lake is a medium-sized lake maintained by the U.S. Army Corps of Engineers. Sanders Cove Park is a Corps campground and picnic area within a two-thousand-acre relict tract of shortleaf pine forest situated on a high bluff overlooking Sanders Creek and the Red River bottoms. The area is open to birdwatchers for no charge, although a fee is charged for camping and other activities.

This island of eastern habitat provides haven to a few eastern species that are largely absent from the surrounding area, including a small population of Pine and Yellow-throated warblers that are breeding in the pines here. Orchard Orioles and Red-headed Woodpeckers are easy to see from the picnic tables. Other breeding species include Eastern Wood-Pewee, Yellow-throated Vireo, White-breasted Nuthatch, and Pileated Woodpecker. The nasal calls of the Fish Crows are common as well. The lake itself is not very birdy, though an occasional Horned Grebe or Common Loon is often present in winter. Recently Texas Parks and Wildlife Department personnel have created a large freshwater marsh below the dam that should harbor a variety of water birds and waterfowl year-round.

LAKE O' THE PINES

P.O. Drawer W
Jefferson, Texas 75657
(903) 665-2336

Lake O' the Pines is located on Little Cypress River a few miles above Caddo Lake, but the two lakes are as different as night and day. They do share many of the same breeding birds, as the surrounding habitat is virtually identical. However, in fall and winter, the deep clear water of Lake O' the Pines attracts hordes of loons and diving ducks as well as gulls and terns. Birders come here expecting to find rarities. Texas' second Yellow-billed Loon was seen here in 1992, and Red-throated and Pacific loons are almost regular each year. Western Grebes, rare in Northeast Texas, are also nearly annual, and the Red-necked Grebe has been recorded. The first Great Black-backed Gull to be seen in Texas away from the Gulf of Mexico was here several ago. There are also records of Sabine's Gull, Thayer's Gull, and Black-legged Kittiwake. Among the several hundred Greater and Lesser Scaup, astute birders often find a White-winged or Surf Scoter and there is a single record of a Black Scoter here, too. Other interesting rarities over the years have included Reddish Egret, Barrow's Goldeneye, Say's Phoebe, and Nelson's Sharp-tailed Sparrow.

NATURE CONSERVANCY PROPERTIES

North Texas Land Steward
The Nature Conservancy of Texas
CR 1140
Celeste, Texas 75423-0463
(903) 568-4139

The Nature Conservancy maintains several natural areas that, although not public land, are of great interest to birders and others concerned with the natural history and geography of Northeast Texas. Perhaps the most impressive is Lennox Woods, a 366-acre tract of virgin old growth pine-oak woodlands in Red River County north of Clarksville. Surrounding forests pale by comparison because the tall ancient trees here look more like those in the Pacific Northwest than like any still found in Texas. Obviously the birds take a back seat to the stunning habitat, but they include nine species of breeding warblers—and deep within the forest there are no cowbirds! This area is little explored in summer, so there may be some surprises waiting to be discovered. Trails have been constructed recently, and the birders are allowed to visit with no appointment. This is a remote area; there are no facilities within ten miles.

The prairies are some of the most beautiful landscapes in Northeast Texas. The best place to experience them is at the Nature

Conservancy's Blackland Prairie Preserve at Clymer Meadow near the town of Celeste. This postage stamp–sized tract preserves the original grasses and wildflowers that once bloomed in profuse abundance on the fertile black soil. The list of plants is impressive, and many are found only on such preserves, so their continued existence is crucial although there are virtually no birds that breed only here. Short-eared Owls are regular in winter—perhaps a lucky visitor will find a Long-eared Owl. This is a premier location for winter sparrows, including Harris's, Fox, White-crowned, and Field sparrows in the brushy thickets, while the Le Conte's Sparrow lurks in the tall grass. You should call ahead to secure permission as the site is not open to the general public.

LAKE FORK RESERVOIR

Located in Wood and Rains counties and managed by the Sabine River Authority, this large lake is the unofficial bass fishing capital of Texas. The lake may be the biggest attraction in all of Northeast Texas, and on any given day hundreds of visitors from around the world are present. It is also one of the most difficult lakes as regards access for birders because the dam is not open to the public and there are no state park facilities. There are still birding opportunities here, however.

One of the most interesting features of the birdlife on the lake is a huge heron and egret colony on Bird Island, near the State Highway 154 bridge between Yantis and Quitman. This island is accessible from Highway 154 via a small Sabine River Authority day-use park on the north side of the lake. In addition to the thousands of Cattle, Snowy, and Great egrets that nest on the island there are about two hundred pairs of Neotropic Cormorants nesting each year, along with a few pairs of Double-crested Cormorants. This is one of the best places in the region to see this diminutive cormorant. A few Anhingas also nest, and small numbers of White Ibis and Tricolored Heron may be breeding as well. Black-bellied Whistling Ducks can be seen here, and in fall look for Wood Storks, Roseate Spoonbills, and other post-breeding wanderers.

Since 1991, a few Tree Swallows have nested in old woodpecker holes in the lake's dead trees. As noted, there are few parks, but a number of private marinas and boat ramps provide access to the lake for viewing. White-breasted Nuthatches are especially common year-round. Most of the Post Oak Savannah breeders are here, such as Eastern Kingbirds and Summer Tanagers. In winter look for rafts of scaup and other diving ducks on the water.

CAMP TYLER

(At Lake Tyler)
For permission to bird here, contact
Alan Byboth at (903) 510-6440

This small property on the edge of Lake Tyler is owned by the Tyler Independent School District and managed by the Camp Tyler Foundation. The property consists of old fields, wooded areas, and second growth brushy scrub. It has proven to be a great place to search for migrants as well as winter sparrows. Among the usual Le Conte's Sparrows that frequent the grassy fields in winter, a Henslow's Sparrow can often be found with a little effort; this is one of the best places in Northeast Texas to see this species. In summer Black-and-white and Pine warblers breed, as do a number of other East Texas birds.

GREENVILLE CITY LAKES

Located off Business U.S. 69 just north of the small community of Peniel, near the Greenville Electric Utilities Power Plant, this collection of small reservoirs is a good place to look for gulls in fall and winter. A note of warning: the dirt roads around them become muddy and impassable for several days after a rain, so be cautious when driving here. Rarities have included Laughing and Sabine's gulls, Black-legged Kittiwakes, and the first Lesser Black-backed Gull seen in Northeast Texas. A few Eared Grebes are always present among the Horned Grebes that overwinter. This is one of the best (and most reliable) places in the region for Hooded Merganser—in recent years almost five hundred have come in at dusk during the winter to spend the night.

CHAPTER 3

Species Accounts

Definition of Terms

The following terms for relative abundance, arranged from most to least frequent in occurrence, are used throughout the book to describe the status of each species.

Abundant: Used to describe a species that occurs widely throughout the area or locally in suitable habitat, frequently in large numbers. This category usually applies to birds that are conspicuous and hard to overlook.

Common: A bird that occurs throughout the region, usually in good numbers. These birds are certain to be seen in proper habitat and season.

Fairly Common: Generally refers to species that do not quite meet the criteria to be considered common. They are often easy to find in suitable habitat at the proper season, though never in large numbers.

Uncommon: Applies to species that, while usually present in proper habitat or at the appropriate season, often occur in small numbers and are sometimes difficult to locate.

Occasional: This term applies to birds that occur somewhat irregularly and are not easy to locate—though their occurrence is not surprising. It often describes species that are either common or uncommon at other times of the season, with small numbers occasionally lingering later than usual.

Rare: Usually refers to species that may occur every year but are sometimes not located regularly. They are generally very local in distribution and must be carefully searched for in proper habitat at the right season.

Very rare: Highly irregular species that have only occurred in the region less than a half dozen times or so. These species are very difficult to locate, though they are expected to occur again.

Accidental: Species with normal range or migratory paths well outside the region. Their occurrence is sometimes attributed to unusual weather or some other unknown phenomena.

The following terms are used to clarify the status of each species in Northeast Texas further on the basis of when and why it occurs in the region.

Resident: Some individuals remain in the region during a particular part of the year. This often refers to summer, winter, or permanent residents.

Migrant: Some individuals migrate through the region, usually on a regular basis.

Post-breeder: A species that wanders into the region, usually fairly regularly, as part of a post-breeding dispersal. This often refers to birds that breed on the Gulf Coast and then wander inland to more productive feeding sites.

Visitor: Presence of the species in the region is not part of a regular migration, although individuals visit occasionally, often during a particular time of year.

Vagrant: A species for which occurrence in the region is not expected. This often describes individuals far out of their species' normal range.

Species Occurring in Northeast Texas

LOONS: FAMILY GAVIIDAE

Red-throated Loon *Gavia stellata*

The Red-throated Loon is a rare migrant and winter visitor to the larger lakes in the region, with records from Lake O' the Pines, Lake Tawakoni, and Cooper Lake. There are about ten records accepted by the TBRC, ranging from early November through late March. Since 1991 this loon has occurred annually in the region, usually in association with Common Loons.

Pacific Loon *Gavia pacifica*

The Pacific Loon is a rare migrant and winter visitor to the region's larger lakes, including Lake Tawakoni, Lake O' the Pines, and Cooper Lake. There are over ten documented records, ranging from late October to early May. Most involve birds in basic or immature plumage, but in late April, 1990, nine birds were present at Lake Tawakoni, including two in breeding plumage.

Common Loon *Gavia immer*

The Common Loon is an uncommon migrant and winter resident on the larger lakes in the region. It is rare and irregular on smaller lakes and ponds, chiefly during migration. In summer it is a rare visitor, with records during June and July at a few locations. The species is most common at Lake Tawakoni and Lake O' the Pines, where over one hundred birds usually spend the winter.

Yellow-billed Loon *Gavia adamsii*

The Yellow-billed Loon is an accidental winter visitor. The only record for the region is from Lake O' the Pines on January 12–14, 1992 (TBRC 1992-23). This individual provided the second documented record for the state.

GREBES: FAMILY PODICIPEDIDAE

Pied-billed Grebe *Podilymbus podiceps*

Pied-billed Grebes are fairly common migrants and winter residents on most of the ponds and lakes throughout the region. During summer they are uncommon to rare residents and may breed when favorable conditions are present. Although individuals are normally solitary, impressive concentrations of several dozen birds are noted occasionally, particularly during fall migration.

1. *The Pied-billed Grebe is a frequent visitor to small lakes and ponds throughout Northeast Texas, where it is often mistaken for a duck. This individual was in Greenville in January, 1999.*

2. Horned Grebes occur on Northeast Texas reservoirs and small lakes during migration and throughout the winter. These were found at the Greenville City Lakes in December, 1996.

3. Although they do not nest in the region, American White Pelicans are present year-round on lakes and reservoirs in Northeast Texas and are most common during migration. This typical congregation was photographed on Cooper Lake in Hopkins County in December, 1997.

4. *Photographed near Greenville in December, 2000, this Black-crowned Night-Heron provided one of the first winter records to be documented in Northeast Texas.*

5. *An adult Glossy Ibis (second from left), seen with White-faced Ibis at Lake Tawakoni in October, 2000, was the first to be photographed in Northeast Texas. Note the dark eye and blue facial skin, traits that help distinguish the species.*

6. Turkey Vultures are common throughout Northeast Texas; these were photographed at Lake Tawakoni in September, 1996. The bird in the rear is drying its wings.

7. (Above) Geese begin their leisurely migration northward through Northeast Texas by mid-January and for the next three months are often observed resting in fields. These Snow and Greater White-fronted Geese were photographed at Big Creek Lake near Cooper in March, 1996.

8. Black Scoters are rarely recorded in Northeast Texas. This female remained for several months at Lake Tawakoni, where she was photographed by David Hurt in December, 1999.

9. *The Red-tailed Hawk is a familiar sight in Northeast Texas. This individual was photographed near Cooper in January, 2001.*

10. *This Semipalmated Plover was photographed at Cooper Lake in April, 1996, during spring migration.*

11. *American Avocets occur during migration around lakes and reservoirs.*

12. *An uncommon migrant, this Ruddy Turnstone was photographed at Cooper Lake in May, 1996.*

13. *An uncommon migrant, this Dunlin in breeding plumage was photographed at Cooper Lake in May, 1996.*

14. *(Below) The Common Snipe is a migrant and winter resident in Northeast Texas. This one was photographed near Cooper in January, 1997.*

15. *Common across Europe and Asia, the Black-headed Gull has recently attempted to colonize parts of North America. This individual spent several winters in a row at Cooper Lake, where it was photographed in January, 1998.*

16. *Bonaparte's Gulls are usually seen around lakes and reservoirs in Northeast Texas and are particularly fond of fishing where water is being discharged, like this immature—identified by the dark barring on the wings—photographed in December, 1998.*

17. *Careful scrutiny has revealed the Common Tern to be a regular migrant to lakes and reservoirs in Northeast Texas. This adult—identified by the blood-red bill and legs—was at Cooper Lake in May, 1997.*

18. *A bird of prairie marshes, lakes, and wetlands, the Black Tern is a migrant to lakes and reservoirs in Northeast Texas. This one was photographed at Cooper Lake in May, 1996.*

19. *This immature Black Skimmer at Lake Tawakoni was one of three present during early August, 1996, strays from the Gulf of Mexico. Speculation is that these birds' unusual presence inland is the result of the previous passage of a hurricane or tropical storm, but no such explanation was available for these birds.*

20. *A stray from South and Central Texas, the Common Ground-Dove is rarely recorded in Northeast Texas. This individual was photographed on a dirt road outside Cooper in May, 1999.*

21. *Scissor-tailed Flycatchers are a common sight, occurring throughout Northeast Texas. This one was photographed at Lake Tawakoni in October, 2000.*

22. *(Below) White-breasted Nuthatches are fairly common breeding residents in wooded areas in Northeast Texas, where they are particularly fond of post oaks. The photograph was taken near Campbell in Hunt County in January, 1997.*

23. *The Rock Wren is a stray from the western United States. The species has been recorded only a few times in Northeast Texas, mainly on the rock riprap of reservoirs, like this individual photographed at Cooper Lake in December, 1996.*

24. *The Bewick's Wren is a migrant and winter resident in Northeast Texas. This individual was photographed near Sulphur Springs on a pile of discarded railroad ties.*

25. American Pipits occur in a variety of habitats in Northeast Texas, from plowed or grassy fields to lake shores and parking lots. This one was photographed at Cooper Lake in March, 1997.

26. Le Conte's Sparrow winters in old fields and pastures throughout Northeast Texas, although this individual was photographed in Dallas in November, 2000.

27. *Eastern Bluebirds are a familiar sight across most of Northeast Texas. This one was photographed in Hunt County in December, 2001.*

28. *A common winter resident in plowed fields during the winter, the Lapland Longspur is often attracted to roadways during snowstorms to feed on seeds. This bird was photographed near Cooper Lake during such a storm in January, 2001.*

29. This well-camouflaged Smith's Longspur was photographed in three-awn grass at Lake Tawakoni in January, 2001. Because these birds blend into their environment so well, they are seldom seen perched on the ground.

30. These Yellow-headed Blackbirds were photographed west of Cooper in May, 1999. Although easily overlooked, these colorful birds are regular during migration in Northeast Texas.

Horned Grebe *Podiceps auritus*

Horned Grebes are common migrants and winter residents on most of the larger lakes in the area. In recent years they have come to be among the most common wintering birds at Cooper Lake and Lake Tawakoni, with several hundred individuals recorded annually. They are usually present from October through April.

Red-necked Grebe *Podiceps grisegena*

The Red-necked Grebe is a very rare migrant and winter visitor. There are five records of the species, ranging from late November through early March. One was at Lake Bob Sandlin, in Titus County, on November 15, 1992 (TBRC 1993-2). Another was at Lake Tawakoni from November 28, 1993 through March 5, 1994 (TBRC 1993-155; TPRF 1204). Two birds were at Wright Patman Reservoir from December 31, 1993, through February 27, 1994 (TBRC 1994-23; TPRF 1221). One was found on the Lake O' the Pines Christmas Bird County on January 2, 1995 (TBRC 1995-11), and one was documented at Cooper Lake on November 28, 1996 (TBRC 1996-163).

Eared Grebe *Podiceps nigricollis*

The Eared Grebe is an uncommon migrant and winter resident of lakes and reservoirs in the region and is much less common in the eastern sections. This species is decidedly less common than the Horned Grebe. The first fall records are usually in early October, though this grebe has been known to arrive by late August. During spring a few may linger until April or May.

Western Grebe *Aechmophorus occidentalis*

The Western Grebe is a very rare migrant and winter visitor to a few of the larger lakes in the region. There are several recent records from Lake O' the Pines and Lake Tawakoni and a single sighting has come from Cooper Lake. Overall, sightings range from early November through early April.

PELICANS: FAMILY PELECANIDAE

American White Pelican *Pelicanus erythrorhynchos*

The American White Pelican is a fairly common migrant and an uncommon to rare localized summer and winter resident on many of the larger lakes in Northeast Texas. There are records for every month of the year.

Brown Pelican *Pelicanus occidentalis*

The Brown Pelican is a very rare visitor in Northeast Texas. There are four recent records of this normally coastal species from the region, three from Lake Tawakoni and one from Lake O' the Pines. All but one have been in fall—there was a very unusual report from Lake Tawakoni on May 16, 1993. There are two fall records from Lake Tawakoni and an undated report from Lake O' the Pines in October, 1992. There is an old report from White Oak Lake, near Sulphur Springs, in October of 1972 or 1973 (Wilson 1986).

CORMORANTS: FAMILY PHALACROCORACIDAE

Neotropic Cormorant *Phalacrocorax brasilianus*

The Neotropic Cormorant is an uncommon summer resident and an irregular winter visitor during mild years. The species is most common on the large reservoirs in the western half of the region. The first spring migrants arrive from late February or early March. They are most common from April through October, though a few often remain until late November or early December. They have nested at Cooper Lake and Lake Tawakoni, but the largest colony is on Bird Island at Lake Fork Reservoir, where more than four hundred pairs have nested in recent years. Numbers of this diminutive cormorant in the region seem to fluctuate somewhat from year to year, although the general trend at many inland locations indicates that they are increasingly common.

Double-crested Cormorant *Phalacrocorax auritus*

Double-crested Cormorants are abundant migrants and winter residents. They are uncommon summer residents—occasionally breeding at a couple of sites. Their numbers have increased dramatically in recent years. The first V-shaped formations from the north begin appearing by mid-August and early September and are often mistaken for early flocks of geese. The birds remain abundant from early October through April, and it is not unusual to observe tens of thousands on most of the largest lakes in the region. There are scattered breeding records from Lake Fork Reservoir and Cooper Lake.

ANHINGAS: FAMILY ANHINGIDAE

Anhinga *Anhinga anhinga*

The Anhinga is an uncommon migrant and summer resident, and a very rare winter visitor, around wooded lakes and reservoirs. It is most common in the eastern sections of the region and irregular and very local in the western areas. A few occasionally linger through the early winter. Anhingas often nest in mixed heron and egret colonies, usually in small numbers.

FRIGATEBIRDS: FAMILY FREGATIDAE

Magnificent Frigatebird *Fregata magnificens*

The Magnificent Frigatebird is an accidental visitor in Northeast Texas. A female or an immature was found at Wright Patman Reservoir following Hurricane Gilbert on October 8, 1988.

HERONS AND EGRETS: FAMILY ARDEIDAE

American Bittern *Botaurus lentiginosus*

The American Bittern is an uncommon to rare migrant in marshes, cattail-lined lakes and ponds, and occasionally in flooded grasses or wet woodlands. Spring migrants occur from March through May and fall migrants occur from August through November. When the weather is mild they may remain all winter in suitable marshy habitat. Additionally, there are several summer records from the Delta County area, although there is no evidence that the species has bred locally.

Least Bittern *Ixobrychus exilis*

The Least Bittern is a rare summer resident in dense cattail marshes. It has been recorded in the region from early April through mid-September. There are no recent sightings of migrants outside typical breeding habitat.

Great Blue Heron *Ardea herodias*

The Great Blue Heron is a common and widespread permanent resident. These very conspicuous herons are found almost wherever there is water, including ponds, streams, flooded fields and ditches, rivers, and lakes. They build large nests sticks placed high atop trees in lakes and in riparian woodlands.

Great Egret *Ardea alba*

Great Egrets are common migrants and summer residents. During winter they are uncommon to rare in the western sections of the region and fairly common in the eastern areas. Spring migrants begin arriving in early March, and most have departed by November. During July and August there is a large post-breeding influx, presumably of birds that bred south of the region.

Snowy Egret *Egretta thula*

The Snowy Egret is a fairly common migrant and summer resident. It becomes more common during midsummer and early fall, when post-breeding wanderers move into the region from the south. There are few records after late October, though the species has been recorded on Christmas Birds Counts a few times in the Longview area.

Little Blue Heron *Egretta caerulea*

The Little Blue Heron is a fairly common migrant and summer resident. The first spring migrants appear in March, and a few immature birds sometimes linger until late October or November. There are also a few December records.

Tricolored Heron *Egretta tricolor*

The Tricolored Heron is a very rare spring migrant and an uncommon post-breeding visitor in midsummer and fall. In late spring and early summer the species is very local in occurrence, but individuals may breed at a few sites. Spring arrivals in April or May are usually adult birds. Immature birds, some of which may have been hatched locally, begin appearing by early July and remain until September or October. There is one December and January record from Wright Patman Reservoir. Two knee-tagged birds that were banded at Cedar Creek Reservoir, in nearby Navarro County, have been found at Cooper Lake. One noted on September 15, 1995, had been banded in early June that year, and another observed on October 4, 1997, had likewise been tagged in June of the same year.

Reddish Egret *Egretta rufescens*

The Reddish Egret is an accidental visitor in Northeast Texas. An immature was at Lake O' the Pines on October 9, 1993. Singles were at Martin Creek Lake in Rusk County on August 4, 1999, and again on September 15, 2000. There is an old report with no details from the Commerce area on September 21, 1947, which Pulich (1988) discounts. There is also an old report for Caddo Lake, on the Karnack Christmas Bird Count in 1958.

Cattle Egret *Bubulcus ibis*

The Cattle Egret is an abundant migrant and summer resident. Numbers have increased in recent decades. There are a few records during winter as well. Breeding colonies are quite large and may contain several thousand pairs of egrets. Spring migrants are detected in March or April. They are usually breeding by late May or June. There is a conspicuous influx in late summer, perhaps consisting of southerly migrating birds that breed to the north: hundreds are regularly encountered in open cattle pastures and around stock ponds in late September and early October. By late October, especially as the weather grows cooler, only scattered flocks are noted. A few linger through November, rarely into December.

Green Heron *Butorides virescens*

The Green Heron is an uncommon summer resident around wooded ponds, creeks, and lakeshores from late March through October.

Black-crowned Night-Heron *Nycticorax nycticorax*

The Black-crowned Night-Heron is an uncommon to rare migrant and summer resident, with records scattered from April through mid-December. Little is known about their status in winter; they may occur locally at that season.

Yellow-crowned Night-Heron *Nyctanassa violacea*

The Yellow-crowned Night-Heron is an uncommon summer resident. Although present from March through October, it is normally very secretive. Immature birds are often conspicuous during August and September and are occasionally seen foraging during the day.

IBISES: FAMILY THRESKIORNITHIDAE

White Ibis *Eudocimus albus*

The White Ibis is an uncommon to rare visitor, chiefly in spring, summer, and fall, though it is locally common in some areas. The species is rare in winter, with just a few reports. The populations of this ibis have increased substantially in recent years, and small flocks of adults in breeding plumage may arrive in April. Breeding is suspected in mixed heron and egret rookeries at Cooper Lake and Lake Fork Reservoir. There are a few records of lingering individuals in winter, primarily during mild years.

Glossy Ibis *Plegadis falcinellus*

The Glossy Ibis is a very rare spring visitor in Northeast Texas. There is a single sight record of two birds at the Texas Eastman Chemical Plant in Longview on April 29, 1996. Two were at Cooper Lake, in Delta County, for several days in August, 2000. Another was photographed at Lake Tawakoni, in Rains County, on October 12, 2000.

White-faced Ibis *Plegadis chihi*

The White-faced Ibis is an uncommon spring and fall migrant. Spring migration stretches from early March through early June, while fall migration extends from mid-July through November. There are a few records for early winter on area Christmas Bird Counts in December.

Roseate Spoonbill *Ajaia ajaja*

The Roseate Spoonbill is an uncommon summer and fall visitor to shallow lakes and ponds throughout the region. Sightings range from late June through October or rarely November. Most records involve one to five birds, though at least twenty birds were present for several days at Lake Tawakoni during late August, 1996.

STORKS: FAMILY CICONIDAE

Wood Stork *Mycteria americana*

The Wood Stork is an uncommon summer and fall post-breeding visitor to the region's artificial reservoirs and wetlands where standing dead trees and shallow water are present. Typically the first arrivals are in late June or July; however, there are recent sightings from the Caddo Lake area in April and May. Most Wood Storks have departed by October, with just a few records from November and even one or two in December. Flocks containing a hundred or more birds are occasionally noted, but most involve considerably fewer. Breeding is suspected at Caddo Lake, though recent aerial surveys to search for nesting evidence have been inconclusive. There are a few old summer records from the 1920s, suggesting that this species may once have bred there.

AMERICAN VULTURES: FAMILY CATHARTIDAE

Black Vulture *Coragyps atratus*

Black Vultures are fairly common permanent residents. They are also conspicuous spring and fall migrants throughout the region. Black Vultures frequently utilize abandoned barns and houses for nesting purposes, and communal roosts are often noted on large electric transmission lines. These vultures are usually outnumbered by Turkey Vultures.

Turkey Vulture *Cathartes aura*
The Turkey Vulture is a common permanent resident and migrant. Although the species is present year-round, there is a noticeable influx of migrants beginning in late September, which continues into November. In spring similar movements are noted in March and April.

SWANS, GEESE, AND DUCKS: FAMILY ANATIDAE

Black-bellied Whistling Duck *Dendrocygna autumnalis*
The Black-bellied Whistling Duck is a rare visitor from spring through fall, with scattered records across the region. The number of sightings seems to have increased in recent years. There are records from late March through late November. The species was recently found breeding just north of the Red River in McCurtain County, Oklahoma.

Fulvous Whistling Duck *Dendrocygna bicolor*
The Fulvous Whistling Duck is a very rare spring visitor. There are two April records, both from Lake Tawakoni: several birds on April 22, 1989, and one in a flooded field below the dam on April 8, 1990.

Greater White-fronted Goose *Anser albifrons*
The Greater White-fronted Goose is a fairly common migrant and an uncommon to rare winter resident. The first flocks are regularly noted after the passage of fall cool fronts in early or mid-October, although a few have been recorded in late September. There is one record from the middle of that month. This is often the first goose species to arrive in fall. Spring migration is from January through March or April.

Snow Goose *Chen caerulescens*
The Snow Goose is a common spring and fall migrant, especially in the western counties of the region. The first fall migrants usually arrive in early October, and movements can be heavy following fall cool fronts well into December. A few Snow Geese are regularly noted on Christmas Bird Counts in the area, but it is not

known if these represent wintering individuals. Spring migration begins early, often by mid-January, and continues through April, with a few lingering until May.

Ross's Goose *Chen rossii*

The Ross's Goose is an uncommon spring and fall migrant, usually seen in large concentrations of Snow Geese. Ross's Geese are much more common on the Blackland Prairie in the western counties than elsewhere in the region and appear to be more common in spring than in fall.

Canada Goose *Branta canadensis*

The Canada Goose is an uncommon spring and fall migrant. Fall migrants begin arriving in October. Not many actually winter in the region, although a few birds can usually be found at that season, making it difficult to determine the onset of spring migration. Most birds have departed by April or early May.

Tundra Swan *Cygnus columbianus*

The Tundra Swan is a very rare fall and winter visitor. There are two old reports in *American Birds,* one in Smith County on December 28, 1963, and the other at Lake O' the Pines sometime in the fall of 1984.

Wood Duck *Aix sponsa*

Wood Ducks are common permanent residents in the region. Boxes erected for them by Texas Parks and Wildlife Department personnel at various sites throughout the region have undoubtedly boosted their numbers in the area. They are much more evident in winter, perhaps due to an influx of migrants or wintering birds of this species.

Gadwall *Anas strepera*

The Gadwall is a common migrant and winter resident on lakes, reservoirs, and ponds of all sizes. The species generally occurs from September through April or May, and there are a few scattered records during the summer months from several locations.

American Wigeon *Anas americana*
The American Wigeon is a common migrant and winter resident. The first fall migrants appear in August, though they are not commonly encountered until September. Most are gone by April or early May.

Mallard *Anas platyrhynchos*
Mallards are common migrants and winter residents throughout the region. They are very local in summer, with breeding records from a handful of locations. Mallards occur in a wide range of aquatic habitats, including flooded pastures and even plowed fields, though in the breeding season they are fond of cattails and other aquatic vegetation.

Mottled Duck *Anas fulvigula*
The Mottled Duck is an uncommon to rare migrant and summer resident, with breeding records from several locations. This species prefers grassy or marshy lakeshores, often where dead timber is available. Most are found from early spring through late fall, with numbers decreasing during the winter, when they are probably rare. These movements, and several recoveries of birds banded along the Gulf Coast, are suggestive of migratory behavior (Stutzenbaker 1988). The Mottled Duck was formerly confined to marshes along the Gulf Coast from South Texas to Florida but has recently staged a well-documented invasion into portions of Kansas, Oklahoma, and Texas. It has been confirmed nesting at Lake Tawakoni and at Lake Bob Sandlin. Most recent reports of the declining American Black Duck in the region are thought to be Mottled Ducks. The Texas Parks and Wildlife Department released over three hundred pen-reared Mottled Ducks at Lake Tawakoni in 1975 and 1976; it is thought that this endeavor was unsuccessful.

Blue-winged Teal *Anas discors*
The Blue-winged Teal is a common spring and fall migrant and a very rare breeding resident. The first fall migrants begin arriving sometime in early to mid-August, occasionally in late July. They do

not become common until September and diminish in numbers in October, with a few lingering until November. In mild winters they may linger into December and are occasionally recorded on Christmas Birds Counts. Spring migrants begin arriving in February or March. They apparently peak in early April and are still numerous by early May. A few linger into June or July, though there are only two breeding records—both from Hunt County.

Cinnamon Teal *Anas cyanoptera*

The Cinnamon Teal is a rare but fairly regular spring migrant within large flocks of Blue-winged Teal in the western counties of the region. The species is very rare elsewhere in Northeast Texas, and its status in fall is unknown. Although Oberholser (1974) indicated a winter record for Bowie County, it likely refers to an early spring migrant in late winter. In spring, conspicuous males have been recorded from mid-February through late April.

Northern Shoveler *Anas clypeata*

Northern Shovelers are common migrants and winter residents on many of the region's lakes and ponds. Fall migration begins sparingly in early or mid-August and increases in September. They remain all winter and begin to depart in April; most are gone by May.

Northern Pintail *Anas acuta*

The Northern Pintail is a fairly common migrant on the lakes and small ponds throughout the region. A few fall migrants begin to appear with other puddle ducks in mid-August, and they become more common in September. A few remain all winter, making the end of fall migration and the beginning of spring migration difficult to judge. Most have gone by April, though a few linger even later—into May.

Green-winged Teal *Anas crecca*

The Green-winged Teal is a common migrant and winter resident. Fall migration begins with a small trickle of birds in August, with larger numbers arriving in September. The birds remain all winter and begin to depart by April and May, though a few may occasionally linger into June or July.

Canvasback *Aythya valisineria*

The Canvasback is a fairly common to uncommon migrant and an uncommon winter resident. The first migrants are usually noted by mid-October with peak numbers occurring in November or later. A few remain through the winter on the larger lakes and ponds. Spring migration probably begins in February and lasts until April or even later on occasion.

Redhead *Aythya americana*

Redheads are uncommon spring and fall migrants. They are generally rare in winter, though small numbers sometimes associate with Ring-necked Ducks or Lesser Scaup. Fall migration begins in late September and October but does not peak until November. Spring migration begins in February and continues through March, though birds occasionally linger into May or even June.

Ring-necked Duck *Aythya collaris*

The Ring-necked Duck is a common migrant and winter resident on lakes and ponds throughout the region. Fall migration generally begins in mid-October. Large numbers remain in the area until March or April, with a few lingering until May.

Greater Scaup *Aythya marila*

Greater Scaup are locally uncommon migrants and are winter residents at a few area lakes, though they are rare to irregular at many others. They are most common at Lake O' the Pines, where several hundred are often present in winter. Good numbers are sometimes found at Lake Bob Sandlin as well. An exceptionally early individual was at Big Creek Lake near Cooper on September 19, 1995; most, however, do not arrive until late October or early November. Most depart by March, though a few have lingered until April or May.

Lesser Scaup *Aythya affinis*
The Lesser Scaup is a common migrant and fairly common winter resident throughout the region. Early migrants begin appearing by late October, larger flocks not being present until November. They remain through the winter and are regularly noted until March, with a few lingering until April or May. A few ragged-looking females and immature birds sometimes remain through summer.

Harlequin Duck *Histrionicus histrionicus*
The Harlequin Duck is an accidental vagrant in Texas, and there is only one record in the region. Harlequin Ducks nest along fast-moving mountain streams and usually winter along rocky shorelines of the Atlantic and Pacific oceans, although a few move inland in winter. The only record in Northeast Texas involves a male and female in winter plumage that were observed at the edge of the Lake Tawakoni spillway, in Van Zandt County, on January 5, 1995 (TBRC 1995-12). The only other record for Texas was a male photographed off South Padre Island from January 30 to February 4, 1989.

Surf Scoter *Melanitta perspicillata*
The Surf Scoter is a very rare migrant and winter visitor. Most records have come from the eastern counties of the region between November and February. Like the other scoters, this species seems to occur most frequently in flocks of scaup.

White-winged Scoter *Melanitta fusca*
The White-winged Scoter is a rare migrant and winter visitor, especially on the larger reservoirs in the eastern portions of the region. There are records from early November through late February.

Black Scoter *Melanitta nigra*
The Black Scoter is a very rare fall migrant and winter visitor. There are four records from the region. One was at Lake O' the Pines from November 18 to 20, 1990. Females were at Lake

Tawakoni, in Van Zandt County, on November 7, 1995, and at Cooper Lake, in Hopkins County, on November 29, 1996. Another was present along the dam at Lake Tawakoni, in Rains and Van Zandt counties, from December 28, 1999, through March, 2000.

Long-tailed Duck *Clangula hyemalis*
The Long-tailed Duck is a rare and irregular winter visitor in Northeast Texas. There are about two dozen records, mostly from October through March. Most of the birds recorded have been present for only a few days, but a female wintered at Lake Tawakoni during winter 1998–99. Most sightings involve one or two birds, though three were found at Lake Tawakoni, in Hunt County, on December 3, 2000.

Bufflehead *Bucephala albeola*
The Bufflehead is a fairly common migrant and winter resident on lakes and ponds throughout the region. It is usually present from late September or early October through late April and early May.

Common Goldeneye *Bucephala clangula*
The Common Goldeneye is an uncommon migrant and winter resident, usually seen in small numbers. A few fall migrants begin arriving in October, with peak numbers occurring in November. The birds depart by March or early April. The largest concentrations typically occur at Lake Tawakoni, where several dozen are regular in winter along the dam.

Barrow's Goldeneye *Bucephala islandica*
The Barrow's Goldeneye is an accidental fall visitor. There are two accepted records in Northeast Texas. Three shot by a duck hunter on a small pond near Greenville on November 6, 1958, provided the first state record for the species (TBRC 1989-202; TPRF 787). One was documented at Lake O' the Pines on November 19–21, 1993 (TBRC 1993-146).

Hooded Merganser *Lophodytes cucullatus*

The Hooded Merganser is a fairly common migrant and winter resident and a rare, localized breeding resident. Birds of this species prefer to forage on small wooded ponds and sloughs during the day, although they roost at night on larger lakes, often in sizable numbers. The first fall arrivals are in mid-October and most have departed by March, though a few have lingered until May or June. There are several recent breeding records from scattered locations in boxes built for Wood Ducks by Texas Parks and Wildlife Department personnel.

Common Merganser *Mergus merganser*

The Common Merganser is a rare and irregular migrant and winter visitor. Most sightings are in December or January though there are records from November through March.

Red-breasted Merganser *Mergus serrator*

The Red-breasted Merganser is an uncommon migrant and winter resident, mostly on the region's larger reservoirs. The species generally occurs in small numbers, though more than three hundred have wintered at Lake Tawakoni in recent years. The first fall arrivals are in October and November. They normally remain until April, with a few seen in May, and there are records for early June.

Ruddy Duck *Oxyura jamaicensis*

The Ruddy Duck is a fairly common migrant and winter resident and a locally rare summer visitor or resident. The bulk of fall migration begins in September and October, and most birds have departed by April or May.

HAWKS, HARRIERS, AND EAGLES: FAMILY ACCIPITRIDAE

Osprey *Pandion haliaetus*

The Osprey is a fairly common migrant and a rare summer and winter visitor. There are records for every month of the year, but migrants are most common from September through November and again from March through May.

Swallow-tailed Kite *Elanoides forficatus*

The Swallow-tailed Kite is a very rare vagrant in the region. The only recent record was at Lake Welch, near Daingerfield, on August 17, 1990. This species may once have been more common in the region and may even have bred. There is an old record without details from Caddo Lake during the summer of 1921 (Cahn 1921).

White-tailed Kite *Elanus leucurus*

The White-tailed Kite is a rare visitor in Northeast Texas. Until recently most records were in late winter and spring, though recently several discoveries of the species have been made in late summer and fall. There are about a dozen records for the area.

Mississippi Kite *Ictinia mississippiensis*

The Mississippi Kite is an uncommon migrant throughout the region and a localized breeding resident in the northern and eastern sections. Spring migration stretches from early April to late May, while fall migration is from late July or early August through late September, rarely into October. Breeding populations are primarily confined to extensively forested areas along the Red and Sulphur rivers south to the Caddo Lake vicinity.

Bald Eagle *Haliaeetus leucocephalus*

The Bald Eagle is a fairly common migrant and winter resident at most area lakes and reservoirs. There are scattered summer sightings from several lakes. The first fall migrants generally arrive in late September. They remain all winter and depart by early March, though there are records for every month of the year.

Northern Harrier *Circus cyaneus*

Northern Harriers are common winter residents in grasslands and agricultural habitats on the Blackland Prairie. They are uncommon elsewhere. Fall migration occasionally begins by early August though most do not arrive until early September—sometimes as late as the middle of that month. They remain in spring until early April, with a few lingering until mid-May.

Sharp-shinned Hawk *Accipiter striatus*
The Sharp-shinned Hawk is a fairly common migrant and an uncommon winter resident. Most records stretch from late August through April or May. Although there are a few summer records, there are no confirmed breeding records for this area, but there are a few breeding records south of the region in the Pineywoods of deep East Texas.

Cooper's Hawk *Accipiter cooperii*
The Cooper's Hawk is an uncommon or fairly common spring and fall migrant and a very low density summer breeding resident. In winter it is an uncommon resident. Because there are records for every month, separating migrants from residents is difficult. Most migration probably occurs from August through November and again from March through May.

Northern Goshawk *Accipiter gentilis*
The Northern Goshawk is an accidental late winter visitor in the region. An immature female was documented west of the small community of Gough in rural Delta County on March 18, 1995 (TBRC 1995-91). Despite several dozen undocumented reports over the past 110 years or more, this was only the ninth accepted record for Texas. There is an unaccepted record from Camp Tyler, in Smith County, on November 14, 1997 (TBRC 1997-159).

Red-shouldered Hawk *Buteo lineatus*
Red-shouldered Hawks are fairly common permanent residents in heavily forested areas, mainly in the eastern half of the region. They are uncommon to rare in the Blackland Prairie, where they are confined to permanently wet riparian areas. They are probably rare to uncommon spring and fall migrants, though it is often difficult to distinguish these from local breeders.

Broad-winged Hawk *Buteo platypterus*
The Broad-winged Hawk is a fairly common migrant and a localized summer resident in large woodlands in the eastern portions

of the region and west along the Red River to Fannin County. Spring migration begins in April and continues through May, with fall migration stretching from late August to October. Breeding birds are found mainly in heavily forested areas. A few dark-morph individuals can usually be found in fall. This rare morph nests only in Alberta and is a rare migrant on the eastern Great Plains. Such dark-morph birds tend to peak in Texas in early October, rather later than the rest of the migrant population.

Swainson's Hawk *Buteo swainsoni*

The Swainson's Hawk is an fairly common migrant in the open areas of the Blackland Prairie and Post Oak Savannah. It is uncommon to rare in the heavily forested eastern counties. In summer, small numbers are usually present in open agricultural habitats, although nesting has not been confirmed.

White-tailed Hawk *Buteo albicaudatus*

The White-tailed Hawk is a accidental winter visitor at Cooper Lake. A dark immature bird, with a distinctive white diamond-shaped patch on the upper breast, was carefully studied in recently burned grassland below the dam at Cooper Lake, in Delta County, on February 15, 1995. The White-tailed Hawk is a bird of coastal grassland and mesquite-oak savannah from Central and South Texas south to South America. It is often seen foraging in burned areas. The Cooper Lake sight record probably represents the most northerly for the United States.

Zone-tailed Hawk *Buteo albonotatus*

The Zone-tailed Hawk is an accidental migrant in Northeast Texas. The only record of this southwestern species involves an adult that was well described, migrating with a large movement of Broad-winged and Swainson's hawks at Lake Tawakoni, in Rains County, on September 21, 2000.

Red-tailed Hawk *Buteo jamaicensis*

The Red-tailed Hawk is a common migrant and winter resident and an uncommon summer breeding resident. Several distinct subspecies inhabit Northeast Texas, and their status and distribution differ. The "Eastern" Red-tailed Hawk, *B. j. borealis,* is an uncommon migrant and a fairly common winter resident. The "Krider's" Red-tailed Hawk, *B. j. kriderii,* is an uncommon to rare, but regular, winter resident—especially in the western portions of the region. The breeding population consists of birds showing characteristics of the "Fuertes" Red-tailed Hawk, *B. j. fuertisi,* of the southwestern United States and Mexico. Birds showing these characteristics are fairly common residents throughout most of the region. The "Western" Red-tailed Hawk, *B. j. calurus,* is a rare to uncommon migrant and winter resident. The much rarer rufous morph has been seen on occasion. The "Harlan's" Hawk, *B. j. harlani,* is an uncommon winter resident, primarily on the Blackland Prairie.

Ferruginous Hawk *Buteo regalis*

The Ferruginous Hawk is a very rare winter visitor, mainly in the open grasslands and farm fields of Delta County. There are about a half dozen records, most involving immature birds, ranging from December to early February. Additionally, there is an early report of an individual in atypical habitat over Caddo Lake on September 30, 1995. An individual banded in Canada was recovered in Titus County in 1995 (Ingold 1995). With more fieldwork, this species may prove to be a regular winter resident in the Blackland Prairie in the western portions of the region.

Rough-legged Hawk *Buteo lagopus*

The Rough-legged Hawk is a very rare and irregular winter visitor. There are only a handful of records in the region, most in midwinter. This species should be identified with caution and carefully separated from unusual variants of the Red-tailed Hawk.

Golden Eagle *Aquila chrysaetos*

The Golden Eagle is a very rare migrant and winter visitor in the region. There are about a dozen regional records, ranging from early October through March. Most have been immature birds, the plumage of which is similar to that of immature Bald Eagles, so this species should be identified with caution.

CARACARAS AND FALCONS: FAMILY FALCONIDAE

Crested Caracara *Caracara plancus*

The Crested Caracara is an uncommon to rare permanent resident in the Post Oak Savannah and Blackland Prairie. Small numbers occur regularly around Lake Tawakoni, in Hunt, Rains, and Van Zandt counties, where breeding is suspected, and north to Hopkins County. Wandering birds are irregular in spring north to Delta County. This area represents the northeastern limit of the species' vast range from Texas into South America.

American Kestrel *Falco sparverius*

American Kestrels are common migrants and winter residents. They are occasional or local summer residents, though little information is available to suggest breeding. Fall migration begins early, often in late July and early August. They become common by early September and remain until March, with a few birds still present in April or May. They are most common and conspicuous in the open country of the Blackland Prairie and the Post Oak Savannah. There are a few scattered June records that may represent breeding birds.

Merlin *Falco columbarius*

The Merlin is an uncommon migrant and a rare winter visitor. The first fall migrants appear in September, usually after the passage of cool fronts. Migration probably continues through November, though there is a slight influx in winter of the subspecies that breeds and winters on the Great Plains—the "Prairie" Merlin.

Spring migration probably extends from March through April or occasionally early May.

Peregrine Falcon *Falco peregrinus*
The Peregrine Falcon is an uncommon to rare migrant and a very rare winter visitor. As Peregrine Falcon populations continue to recover after being nearly wiped out of eastern North America, sightings of migrants will likely continue to increase in the region. Fall migration begins in August and continues well into December. The bulk of the spring migration extends from March through May.

Prairie Falcon *Falco mexicanus*
The Prairie Falcon is a very rare migrant. There are about a half dozen records from the western counties of the region, ranging in fall from mid-September through December. There are two sight records from the Caddo National Grasslands Christmas Bird Count. The single spring record is for early March from Hunt County.

PHEASANTS: FAMILY PHASIANIDAE

Wild Turkey *Meleagris gallopova*
Naturally occurring Wild Turkeys may still occur in the extreme eastern portions of the region. During the 1990s Wild Turkeys from Missouri were introduced at selected locations by Texas Parks and Wildlife Department personnel.

QUAIL: FAMILY ODONTOPHORIDAE

Northern Bobwhite *Colinus virginianus*
The Northern Bobwhite is an uncommon permanent resident in old fields, cattle pastures, and brushy areas adjacent to woods. The species' numbers seem to have declined in recent years, perhaps in response to predation by the introduced fire ant.

RAILS, GALLINULES, AND COOTS: FAMILY RALLIDAE

King Rail *Rallus elegans*
The King Rail is a rare, irregular, and very localized summer resident in marshy habitats. It occurs from early April through mid-

September. The only confirmed breeding records are from Big Creek Lake. The status of the King Rail in the region is difficult to assess due to the secretive nature of the species. Despite the limited amount of marshy habitat available, King Rails are easily overlooked and no doubt occur on a more regular basis than is currently known.

Virginia Rail *Rallus limicola*

The Virginia Rail is a rare to uncommon migrant and winter resident in marshes and wet grassy fields. As in the case of the King Rail, this species is secretive, which makes assessing its status difficult. There are records from late September though mid-May.

Sora *Porzana carolina*

Soras are fairly common migrants and rare winter visitors or residents. They will accept almost any type of wet grassy habitat, including cattails, flooded grasses, wet ditches, and occasionally dry grassy shoreline or pastures. Most are recorded from September through November and again in April and May. A single summer record at Cooper Lake on August 2, 1994, is thought to represent an early fall migrant.

Purple Gallinule *Porphyrula martinica*

The Purple Gallinule is a rare and very localized summer resident or visitor in wooded lakes and ponds with dense wetland plants. Most recent sightings have been from the eastern sections of the region. Overall, records range from April through late September.

Common Moorhen *Gallinus chloropus*

The Common Moorhen is a rare, irregular, and localized spring migrant and summer visitor, with records from late April through late September. There are breeding records from the Grand Saline marsh in June, 1990, and from the Little Sandy Hunting Club in Wood County in 1992.

American Coot *Fulica americana*

American Coots are common to abundant migrants and winter residents on most large ponds and lakes. In summer they are localized residents in wet marshy habitats. Although there are records for every month of the year, the larger fall influx begins in September. The birds remain abundant through April, with a few lingering until late May or early June.

CRANES: FAMILY GRUIDAE

Sandhill Crane *Grus canadensis*

The Sandhill Crane is a rare migrant in Northeast Texas. There are only about a half dozen records. Spring records are from early March through mid-April, while fall records are mainly from late October through late November. Oberholser (1974) cites a summer report without details for Bowie County. Sandhill Cranes are fairly common during migration as close as the Dallas–Fort Worth area.

PLOVERS: FAMILY CHARADRIIDAE

Black-bellied Plover *Pluvialis squatarola*

The Black-bellied Plover is a rare spring and an uncommon fall migrant. Spring migration is from March through May and fall migration is from July through November.

American Golden-Plover *Pluvialis dominica*

The American Golden Plover is an uncommon to fairly common spring migrant. It is especially fond of cattle pastures and plowed fields, although it occasionally occurs along shores in typical shorebird fashion. In fall this species is a rare but regular migrant. Spring migration begins in early or mid-March but does not peak until the latter part of that month and into early April. A few are still passing through in early May, rarely into the middle of May. Fall migration is from mid-August through early December.

Snowy Plover *Charadrius alexandrinus*

The Snowy Plover is a rare spring and fall migrant, chiefly in the western counties. There are about eleven regional records—all since

1990. Spring migrants have been recorded from early March through mid-May, while those in fall have been from July through late September.

Semipalmated Plover *Charadrius semipalmatus*
The Semipalmated Plover is fairly common migrant and a very rare winter visitor. Spring migration stretches from early April through late May. Fall migration is usually from mid-July though November. An individual lingered until late December, 1991, at the Texas Eastman Chemical Plant near Longview.

Piping Plover *Charadrius melodus*
The Piping Plover is a rare fall migrant and a very rare spring migrant. Fall migrants are recorded from July through September. There are only a few spring records, mostly from late April through mid-May.

Killdeer *Charadrius vociferus*
The Killdeer is a common and widespread permanent resident. This well-known bird breeds in a variety of habitats, including cattle pastures, lakeshores, grassy medians along highways, urban parks and parking lots, and similar settings. It forages in many of the same areas and is frequently found in plowed fields and along roadways, sometimes in the road itself.

Mountain Plover *Charadrius montanus*
The Mountain Plover is a very rare spring migrant in the Blackland Prairie. There are four records, including one in Van Zandt County in early April, 1987, and three from Delta County, all in large open fields. Eleven were in a fallow field a few yards north of Cooper Lake on March 19, 1994. Two were in a bare field near the community of Racetrack on March 11, 1995. Two others were found in a burned pasture several miles west of Cooper on April 8, 1995.

AVOCETS AND STILTS: FAMILY RECURVIROSTRIDAE

Black-necked Stilt *Himantopus mexicanus*

The Black-necked Stilt is a rare migrant and a very rare breeding resident. Most of the dozen or so records have been in the western counties of the region, though there is one record for Harrison County in the east. Spring migrants have been recorded from mid-April to late May. The only fall records are during September. A pair raised two young in a cattail marsh on private property near Grand Saline, in Van Zandt County, in August, 1990, the only nesting record for Northeast Texas.

American Avocet *Recurvirostra americana*

The American Avocet is a fairly common migrant in the western half of the region and uncommon to rare in the eastern half. Spring migrants occur from early March through late May, while fall migrants occur from early July (there is one mid-June record from Cooper Lake) through early November. A high total of ninety-three birds was noted at Cooper Lake on October 16, 1997.

WOODCOCK, SNIPE, AND SANDPIPERS: FAMILY SCOLOPACIDAE

Greater Yellowlegs *Tringa melanoleuca*

The Greater Yellowlegs is a common migrant and an uncommon winter resident throughout the region. There are records for every month of the year. Fall migrants begin arriving in late June and continue through November or December. A few spend the winter. Northbound birds move through from March through late May or early June.

Lesser Yellowlegs *Tringa flavipes*

The Lesser Yellowlegs is a common migrant and a rare to uncommon winter visitor. Fall migrants are heading south by late June and continue through November, although there are a few records on Christmas Bird Counts in December. Spring migration is mostly during March, April, and May.

Solitary Sandpiper *Tringa solitaria*
The Solitary Sandpiper is an uncommon migrant in a variety of habitats, including lakes, small farm ponds, and flooded grasslands and fields. It is generally absent in winter, though there is a recent December record from Longview. Spring migration extends from March through May, and fall migration is from early July through early November.

Willet *Catoptrophorus semipalmatus*
The Willet is an uncommon to rare migrant. Fall migration extends from late June through October. Spring migration is from March through May. Most sightings involve one or two birds, but a phenomenal fifty-two were found resting on the bank of a small pond near Campbell, in Hunt County, on April 27, 1992.

Spotted Sandpiper *Actitis macularia*
The Spotted Sandpiper is a fairly common migrant in a variety of wetland habitats, including marshes, shorelines, and the rocky embankments at the region's artificial reservoirs. Spring migration stretches from March through May, while fall migration is from late June through November. A few can usually be found in winter at most of the large lakes.

Upland Sandpiper *Bartramia longicauda*
The Upland Sandpiper is a fairly common migrant. Migrants are often heard at night or early in the morning as they fly overhead. They prefer short grass pastures, plowed fields, and dry shoreline. The first spring arrivals are in early March and the species grows more common by the later part of that month and into April, continuing through May. Fall migration may begin occasionally by late June and increases in mid-July. Small numbers occur daily, especially in the western sections of the region, through October, with a few lingering birds still moving through in early November. There are a couple of mid-June records in the Blackland Prairie in Hunt and Delta counties, but there is no evidence of breeding.

Whimbrel *Numenius phaeopus*

The Whimbrel is a rare spring and very rare fall migrant. There are six spring records—all in 1999 and 2000—ranging from early to late May. A maximum of ten birds were at Cooper Lake on May 19, 2000. There are two fall records, one at Lake Bob Sandlin on September 29, 1990, and another photographed at Lake Tawakoni on August 3, 1996.

Long-billed Curlew *Numenius americanus*

The Long-billed Curlew is a very rare migrant and winter visitor in Northeast Texas. There are nine regional records, which reveal no clear pattern of occurrence. Four are fall records—one near Lake O' the Pines on September 20, 1975, and three at Cooper Lake, where singles were noted on August 27–28, 1998; August 27, 1999; and September 3, 2000. There are also three winter records, for singles at Lake Tawakoni on December 18, 1992, and February 6, 1994, and at Texas Eastman Chemical Plant, in Harrison County, on December 23, 2000. There are two spring records: at Lake Tawakoni, in Rains County, on April 5, 1997, and at Lake Bob Sandlin on April 14, 1990.

Hudsonian Godwit *Limosa haemastica*

The Hudsonian Godwit is an uncommon but fairly regular spring migrant to shallow wetlands, mudflats, and grassy lakeshores. It is an accidental fall migrant. Small numbers are routinely encountered in the region in spring from early April through late May. There is a single fall record from Texas Eastman Chemical Plant near Longview on November 1, 1992.

Marbled Godwit *Limosa fedoa*

The Marbled Godwit is a very rare spring migrant and a rare fall migrant. The dozen or so fall records range from late June to mid-September. There are only two spring records, one at Lake Bob Sandlin April 14, 1990, and one at Cooper Lake, on April 16, 1998.

Ruddy Turnstone *Arenaria interpres*

The Ruddy Turnstone is a very rare and irregular spring migrant and a rare fall migrant. There are less than a half dozen spring records—all in May. Fall sightings range from late July through early October. Ruddy Turnstones prefer shorelines of the area's larger lakes.

Red Knot *Calidris canutus*

The Red Knot is a very rare migrant in Northeast Texas. There are two records—one in spring and one in fall. The fall record was at Lake Tawakoni on August 30, 1996. The spring record was in a small wetland on private property near Grand Saline, in Van Zandt County on April 28, 1995.

Sanderling *Calidris alba*

The Sanderling is rare in spring migration and uncommon, though regular, in fall. Sanderlings prefer the shorelines of the large lakes. There are spring records from early April through late May and fall records from mid-July through October.

Semipalmated Sandpiper *Calidris pusilla*

Semipalmated Sandpipers are fairly common to common migrants. They are usually outnumbered by Least Sandpipers, with which they often associate. Spring migrants are found from late March through late May, while fall sightings range from late June through October.

Western Sandpiper *Calidris mauri*

The Western Sandpiper is an uncommon to fairly common migrant and a rare winter visitor. Fall migration begins in late June or early July and continues until November, though late lingering individuals are occasionally noted into December or January.

Least Sandpiper *Calidris minutilla*

The Least Sandpiper is a common migrant and an uncommon winter resident. It occurs in a variety of wetland habitats, including lakeshores, wet ditches, and moist plowed fields. Fall migrants return by late June, with larger numbers arriving by mid-July. They remain common into December or later. By March there is an influx of birds from the south, with spring migrants continuing through early June. Small flocks are regular throughout winter where suitable habitat is available.

White-rumped Sandpiper *Calidris fuscicollis*

White-rumped Sandpipers are common spring migrants. They are late migrants, often not detected until late April or early May. Migration peaks in mid-May and continues into mid-June. There is one fall record—an adult in faded breeding plumage at Cooper Lake on July 18, 1999.

Baird's Sandpiper *Calidris bairdii*

The Baird's Sandpiper is an uncommon but regular migrant. It occurs in spring from early April through late May and in fall from early July through late October.

Pectoral Sandpiper *Calidris melanotos*

Pectoral Sandpipers are common migrants. They occur in a wide variety of habitats, from plowed fields to lakeshores to flooded fields. Migrants have been recorded in spring from late February through late May and in fall from late June through December.

Dunlin *Calidris alpina*

The Dunlin is an uncommon migrant and a rare winter visitor. Dunlins are most common during fall, occurring mainly in October and November. During mild weather it is not unusual to find one or two along the shore on area lakes. They are irregular in spring throughout most of the region, though they appear to be regular from early March through late May at Cooper Lake and Lake Tawakoni, with peak daily counts often in double digits.

Stilt Sandpiper *Calidris himantopus*
The Stilt Sandpiper is an uncommon to locally common migrant. It occurs in fall from early July through mid-November. Spring migration is from March through May.

Buff-breasted Sandpiper *Tryngites subruficollis*
The Buff-breasted Sandpiper is a fairly common migrant in dry fields and pastures, on dry shoreline, and on exposed mudflats. Unlike most shorebirds, these birds are seldom seen in the water. They occur in spring from early April through late May and in fall from mid-July through late October.

Short-billed Dowitcher *Limnodromus griseus*
The Short-billed Dowitcher is an uncommon to fairly common migrant. Its status is probably partly clouded by identification difficulties, as it closely resembles the Long-billed Dowitcher. The Short-billed species was once thought to be rare in spring, but there are several photographic records of *L. g. hendersoni* from Cooper Lake in May. The birds probably occur more widely as uncommon migrants from late April through late May. During fall, Short-billed Dowitchers occur from early July through mid-October.

Long-billed Dowitcher *Limnodromus scolopaceus*
The Long-billed Dowitcher is a fairly common migrant in small numbers and a rare to locally uncommon winter resident. Many of the comments for Short-billed Dowitcher apply to this species as well. Fall migrants seem to arrive a bit later than Short-billed Dowitchers, usually in mid- to late July. They remain until November or December, though a few can usually be seen all winter. Spring migrants begin arriving in February or March and continue through May.

Common Snipe *Gallinago gallinago*
The Common Snipe is a fairly common migrant and winter resident in a variety of wet habitats, including wet or plowed fields, lakeshores, road ditches, and any ephemeral wetlands. Fall migra-

tion begins in late August and early September; there is one exceptionally early record from Cooper Lake on July 26, 1998. The birds remain all winter, though there is an influx of migrants in March and April. A few linger until mid-May.

American Woodcock *Scolopax minor*
The American Woodcock is an uncommon to fairly common winter resident in clear-cuts and second growth woodlands in the eastern half of the region. It is a very rare summer visitor, and there are a few scattered breeding records as well. The species is rare to uncommon in the western half of the region, where it occurs chiefly from late October through early May.

Wilson's Phalarope *Phalaropus tricolor*
The Wilson's Phalarope is a fairly common migrant. There are fall records from late June through early October. The bulk of spring migration is in April and May.

Red-necked Phalarope *Phalaropus lobatus*
The Red-necked Phalarope is a very rare regional migrant. There are three recent records, one in spring and two in fall. An adult male in slightly faded breeding plumage was photographed at Cooper Lake during its stay from July 18 to 20, 1998, followed by another at that location on July 6, 1999. The only spring record is from the Grand Saline marsh on April 16, 1995.

Red Phalarope *Phalaropus fulicaria*
The Red Phalarope is an accidental spring migrant in the region. An adult male molting into breeding plumage was photographed at Cooper Lake on May 11, 1996 (TBRC 1996-73). This record represents only the third accepted spring record for Texas.

GULLS, KITTIWAKES, AND TERNS: FAMILY LARIDAE

Pomarine Jaeger *Stercorarius pomarinus*
The Pomarine Jaeger is a very rare fall migrant at Cooper Lake. The only record involves an adult or subadult that was documented

as it harassed several Ring-billed Gulls and Forster's Terns at Pelican Point on October 3, 1992. A large dark jaeger seen there on September 24–26, 1998, was probably this species.

Parastic Jaeger *Stercorarius parasiticus*
The Parasitic Jaeger is a rare fall migrant and an accidental winter visitor. One was photographed at Lake Tawakoni on August 12, 1996. Another was seen harassing a Ring-billed Gull at Cooper Lake on November 7–9, 1997. Two were at Lake Tawakoni from November 14 to 16, 1999. An adult carefully studied at Lake Tawakoni on January 21, 2001, provides one of the few winter records anywhere inland in North American at that season.

Long-tailed Jaeger *Stercorarius longicaudus*
The Long-tailed Jaeger is a very rare fall migrant. There are two records from region—an adult at Lake Tawakoni on November 5, 1996 (TBRC 1996-162), and a light-morph immature on September 10, 2000.

Laughing Gull *Larus atricilla*
Laughing Gulls are uncommon but regular spring through fall visitors to Cooper Lake and Lake Tawakoni. Elsewhere they are less common. In winter they are rare visitors, with scattered sightings from several locations. There are now more than seventy-five records of this primarily coastal species in the region.

Franklin's Gull *Larus pipixcan*
The Franklin's Gull is a common spring and a common to abundant fall migrant. It is a very rare winter visitor or straggler and an uncommon to rare summer visitor. Although a few nonbreeding individuals are regularly recorded in summer and early fall, the first big wave of migrants does not occur until late October and early November. During the peak of fall migration, it is not unusual to observe several thousand Franklin's Gulls in one day—especially in the western counties of the area. They begin to diminish in late November and a few linger until early or mid-December or later.

One or two sometimes occur in late February. However, the first real migratory movements do not occur until late March or early April. These gulls are somewhat irregular in spring—in some years large flocks are recorded, and in other years few birds are seen. They are usually gone by late May, but a few occasionally linger until June.

Little Gull *Larus minutus*
The Little Gull is a very rare fall migrant and winter visitor to Wright Patman Reservoir and Cooper Lake, with a total of four accepted records. The first area record was at Wright Patman Reservoir on January 29, 1992 (TBRC 1992-38). A second-winter bird at Cooper Lake that was seen briefly on October 10, 1992, and documented poorly, was not accepted (TBRC 1992-170). An adult in winter plumage was seen at the same location on February 13, 1993 (TBRC 1993-65). Another was at Wright Patman Reservoir from December 31, 1993, through February 18, 1994 (TBRC 1994-22; TPRF 1222). A first-winter bird was photographed at Cooper Lake during its stay from December 6 to 12, 1996 (TBRC 1996-188).

Black-headed Gull *Larus ridibundus*
The Black-headed Gull is a rare migrant and very localized winter resident in Northeast Texas. Since 1993 the species has occurred annually and may prove to be regular in large flocks of Bonaparte's Gulls. There are five regional records, ranging from late October to late March. There are multiple records from Wright Patman Reservoir and Cooper Lake and a single record came from Lake Tawakoni on December 10, 1995 (TBRC 1995-193). At Wright Patman one was present from January 2 to 20, 1993 (TBRC 1993-35). What may have been the same bird returned on December 31, 1993, and remained until February 18, 1994 (TBRC 1994-31: TPRF 1223). Another was there on December 28, 1996 (TBRC 1997-3). At Cooper Lake there are records from February 12 to March 25, 1996 (TBRC 1996-20). The next fall one was there from November 11, 1996, until February 13, 1997 (TBRC 1996-161), which

returned October 26, 1997, through February, 1998, (TBRC 1997-162) and again from November 18, 1998, through February, 1999 (TBRC 1998-pending).

Bonaparte's Gull *Larus philadelphia*
The Bonaparte's Gull is a fairly common migrant and winter resident at most of the larger reservoirs in Northeast Texas, though it is uncommon to rare at the smaller ones. A few Bonaparte's Gulls usually arrive in late October, although they do not become numerous until mid-November or later. They peak from late November through early February and are still fairly common in March, with a few lingering into April or mid-May.

Ring-billed Gull *Larus delawarensis*
The Ring-billed Gull is a common migrant and winter resident at most of the region's lakes and reservoirs. It is an uncommon to rare localized summer visitor to a few large area lakes. In general the first fall arrivals are in late July, though recently a few have begun remaining all summer in some areas. They are often common by late August, their numbers continuing to increase well into winter. They begin to disappear in April and May.

California Gull *Larus californicus*
The California Gull is a very rare winter and spring visitor. There are three regional records. The initial record for the region is a first-winter bird found in a gull roost at Cooper Lake from February 20 through March 5, 1996 (TBRC 1996-48). One was at Lake Tawakoni on December 25, 1997, and one was photographed at Cooper Lake in May, 1999.

Herring Gull *Larus argentatus*
The Herring Gull is an uncommon migrant and winter resident at the area's larger lakes and reservoirs, always in small numbers. In general the first fall migrants arrive in September and remain until April, though there are several recent summer records from Lake Tawakoni and Cooper Lake.

Thayer's Gull, *Larus thayeri*

The Thayer's Gull is a very rare winter visitor. A first-winter Thayer's Gull was carefully studied and photographed near the discharge tower at Cooper Lake, in Hopkins County, from December 23, 1994, through March 5, 1995 (TBRC 1995-39). One was at Lake O' the Pines on November 23, 1996 (TBRC 1996-159; TPRF 1525). Another was at Lake Tawakoni on December 5, 1996 (TBRC 1996-189). A fourth was documented at Cooper Lake, in Hopkins County, on October 7, 2000.

Lesser Black-backed Gull *Larus fuscus*

The Lesser Black-backed Gull is an accidental or very rare visitor in Northeast Texas. Until the winter of 2000–2001, there were no regional records of this Old World gull, which has recently colonized parts of North America. The first was an adult at the Greenville City Lakes, in Hunt County, on December 10, 2000, followed by another adult at Lake Tawakoni on January 12, 2001, and a first-year bird there in January, 2001.

Glaucous Gull *Larus hyperboreus*

The Glaucous Gull is a very rare fall migrant in Northeast Texas. The only records are from Lake Tawakoni, including a first-winter bird photographed on November 29–30, 1997, and a second-year bird from January 2 to early March, 2001.

Great Black-backed Gull *Larus dominicanus*

The Great Black-backed Gull is an accidental winter visitor. A third-winter Great Black-backed Gull found at the Texas Eastman Chemical Plant in Longview on December 30, 1992, was relocated on January 3, 1993, at Lake O' the Pines, where it remained until March 27 (TBRC 1993-4; TPRF 1144). This bird provided the first inland record for Texas.

Sabine's Gull *Xema sabini*

The Sabine's Gull is a rare fall migrant, primarily to the larger lakes in the area. There are eight records of this pelagic gull in the region, all since 1994. Most birds occur in September and October, though there are records from late August through late December. Most involve immature birds but there are at least two records of adults.

Black-legged Kittiwake *Rissa tridactyla*

The Black-legged Kittiwake is a very rare late fall and early winter visitor. There are six accepted records, all between late November and late December. The first, at Lake O' the Pines on December 1, 1990 (TBRC 1990-152), was followed by others at Lake Bob Sandlin from November 18 to 25, 1995 (TBRC 1995-152); Lake Tawakoni on December 25–26, 1995 (TBRC 1996-3; TPRF 1446); Cooper Lake, November 23, 1996 (TBRC 1996-164); Wright Patman Reservoir, November 30, 1996 (TBRC 1996-155; TPRF 1484); and Greenville City Lakes, December 1–2, 1996 (TBRC 1996-165).

Caspian Tern *Sterna caspia*

The Caspian Tern is a fairly common migrant and summer visitor. Caspian Terns are regular spring and fall migrants to Cooper Lake, somewhat more common in fall. Generally fewer than fifteen or twenty birds are present; however, on September 17, 1994, a phenomenal ninety birds were observed at Cooper Lake. Southbound migrants sometimes appear as early as late July. During the summer of 1994, up to five birds were present during June and July.

Royal Tern *Sterna maxima*

The Royal Tern is an accidental summer visitor. There are three summer records of this coastal bird in the region. The first involved a pair in breeding plumage at Cooper Lake on June 25, 1994. Two additional records are from Lake Tawakoni, where one was found on August 8, 1996, followed by one in basic plumage that was photographed during its stay from June 23 through July 11, 1998.

Roseate Tern *Sterna dougallii*

The Roseate Tern is an accidental visitor. There is one well-documented sight record in the region. On June 25, 1995, an adult, accompanied by a half dozen Forster's Terns, was studied at length at Cooper Lake. This extraordinary record was accepted by the Texas Bird Records Committee as only the second for the state (TBRC 1995-92).

Common Tern *Sterna hirundo*

The Common Tern is an uncommon migrant and a rare summer visitor. Several recent summer records at Lake Tawakoni and Cooper Lake make distinguishing fall migrants from summer visitors difficult. There are several records of birds present by August, though they are more common in September and October, with one or two late records in November. Spring sightings are largely in April and May.

Forster's Tern *Sterna forsteri*

The Forster's Tern is a common migrant and winter resident, with records for every month of the year. A few nonbreeding birds are usually present in summer on the region's larger reservoirs, and by late June and early July they often number in the hundreds at both Lake Tawakoni and Cooper Lake.

Least Tern *Sterna antillarum*

The Least Tern is an uncommon to rare spring and fall migrant and very localized breeding resident. Confirmed breeding records have come from Lake Tawakoni and Cooper Lake; the birds probably also nest on sandbars in the Red River. Rarely, spring migrants arrive in April, most passing through from May through early June. Fall migrants likely occur from July through late September or occasionally early October.

Sooty Tern *Sterna fuscata*

The Sooty Tern is an accidental visitor to large lakes in Northeast Texas. There are two regional records of this highly pelagic tern, both following hurricanes. The first was an immature described from Lake O' the Pines on August 26, 1992, following Hurricane Andrew's encounter with the Louisiana coast. An adult Sooty Tern was at Cooper Lake on August 3, 1995, two days after Hurricane

Dean tracked inland though West Texas. The bird appeared healthy and was quite approachable; it could not be found the next day.

Black Tern *Chlidonias niger*
The Black Tern is a fairly common migrant. In summer nonbreeders are rare and irregular lingering residents, especially at Lake Tawakoni and Cooper Lake. Spring migrants generally occur from April through June and fall migrants from late July through October.

Black Skimmer *Rynchops niger*
The Black Skimmer is a very rare spring and summer visitor. There are four records of this coastal bird in the region, three from Lake Tawakoni and one from Cooper Lake. The Lake Tawakoni records consist of one on May 15, 1988, that was joined the next day by a second bird; another on July 8, 1990; and three immature birds photographed during their stay from August 5 to 9, 1996. On June 27, 1998, an adult was photographed at Cooper Lake.

PIGEONS AND DOVES: FAMILY COLUMBIDAE

Rock Dove *Columbia livia*
Rock Doves are fairly common permanent residents in urban areas and around barns, farmhouses, grain silos, feedlots, and similar habitats. They often nest on rooftops and under bridges and overpasses.

Eurasian Collared-Dove *Streptopelia decaocto*
The Eurasian Collared-Dove is an exotic species introduced in the Bahamas, whence it spread to Florida during the mid-1980s. Since then its numbers have exploded in North America and the birds are rapidly expanding their range north and west across the continent. They were first recorded in the region near Texarkana in 1995. Additional populations have been discovered at several other locations. In a few years Eurasian Collared-Doves will likely be common throughout the region.

White-winged Dove *Zenaida asiatica*
The White-winged Dove has recently become a rare visitor in the region. Vagrants from the rapidly expanding populations in South and Central Texas occur in the western sections of the region, primarily in spring, though there are a few records from the eastern Pineywoods in winter. The birds are most frequently encountered in urban areas.

Mourning Dove *Zenaida macroura*
The Mourning Dove is a common permanent resident in a variety of habitats throughout the area.

Inca Dove *Columbina inca*
The Inca Dove is a locally uncommon to rare resident, primarily in cities and towns. The species is rapidly expanding its range northward through Texas. These doves are especially fond of birdseed thrown on the ground and frequently visit bird feeders as well.

Common Ground-Dove *Columbina passerina*
The Common Ground-Dove is a rare visitor in the region during all seasons, being least common in spring and summer. Most records are between September and February, a time when small numbers often wander well north of their normal range in Central and southern Texas. This dove may be a rare, irregular summer resident in the extreme southeastern portion of the region; there is a recent May record from Delta County.

CUCKOOS, ROADRUNNERS, AND ANIS: FAMILY CUCULIDAE

Black-billed Cuckoo *Coccyzus erythropthalmus*
The Black-billed Cuckoo is a rare migrant, primarily in spring. Spring migrants have been recorded from mid-April through mid-May. Fall records are very rare and range from late August through mid-September.

Yellow-billed Cuckoo *Coccyzus americanus*
The Yellow-billed Cuckoo is a fairly common summer resident and migrant throughout the region. It occurs from early April through October or rarely early November.

Greater Roadrunner *Geococcyx californianus*
Greater Roadrunners are an uncommon permanent resident in the region. They are most common in the Blackland Prairie and the Post Oak Savannah, where they prefer dense brushy areas adjacent to roads, cattle pastures, or other open areas. In the east they occur locally in second growth woodlands and clear-cuts.

Groove-billed Ani *Crotophaga sulcirostris*
The Groove-billed Ani is a very rare late summer and fall visitor. There are three records, ranging from early September through mid-October. The first was near Douglassville, in Cass County, on October 11, 1972. Another was observed at Big Creek Lake in Delta County on September 4, 1993, followed by one at Cooper Lake, also in Delta County, on October 2, 1994.

BARN OWLS: FAMILY TYTONIDAE

Barn Owl *Tyto alba*
The Barn Owl is a locally uncommon to rare permanent resident, largely in old houses and barns, especially in the Blackland Prairie. In addition these owls often roost in winter in eastern red cedars. In the eastern sections of the region they are probably localized residents in urban areas.

TYPICAL OWLS: FAMILY STRIGIDAE

Eastern Screech Owl *Otus asio*
Eastern Screech Owls are uncommon to locally common permanent residents. They appear to be more common in the forested sections in the east, though they probably occur throughout the region, especially in urban areas.

Great Horned Owl *Bubo virginianus*
The Great Horned Owl is a common permanent resident. It breeds in a variety of open and brushy habitats.

Burrowing Owl *Athene cunicularia*
The Burrowing Owl is a very rare visitor in Northeast Texas but may have once occurred more frequently. Due to recent rapid declines in the population of this species, since 1940 there have been only three records. The Burrowing Owl was first reported in Northeast Texas during the 1930s in Hunt County. Delbert Tarter (1940) considered it a rare winter resident in the Commerce area and listed records from November 21 through April 21. One was found sitting on a fence post in a peach tree orchard between Flint and Noonday in Smith County on April 7, 1963. One was discovered roosting in a pipe in a parking lot at the Lone Star Steel Plant in Morris County, where it was seen from November 15 to 27, 1985. The most recent record came from Lake Tawakoni in Rains County, where a migrant was photographed on October 16, 2000. This bird was flushed from a roost in a trash pile. Oberholser (1974) cites a questionable sighting from Fannin County.

Barred Owl *Strix varia*
The Barred Owl is a fairly common permanent resident in mature woodlands and river bottoms. It is absent from many parts of the Blackland Prairie except along large wooded streams.

Long-eared Owl *Asio otus*
The Long-eared Owl is probably a rare irregular visitor or winter resident, although its status remains unclear. There are two recent reports from Delta County and a series of sightings from Lake Tyler in the 1970s. In December, 1999, one was observed several times roosting in a cedar tree at the Nature Conservancy's Clymer Meadow west of Celeste, in Hunt County. Oberholser (1974) cites a fall record without details for Red River County.

Short-eared Owl *Asio flammeus*

The Short-eared Owl is a rare to locally uncommon migrant and winter resident in large grasslands in the Blackland Prairie and very locally in reclaimed strip mines in the eastern sections of the region. Elsewhere, it is a very rare and irregular migrant. These owls are sometimes quite numerous in prime habitat, although in most years only two or three are seen. In the winter of 1995–96 between thirty-five and forty birds were present in one large field near Cooper, just north of State Highway 64. Pulich (1988) indicates that forty were shot illegally by a poacher in Lamar County on January 1, 1981. Outside the Blackland Prairie they are rare and irregular—Oberholser (1974) cites only two winter records without details for Marion and Smith counties. Recent records have come from the Sabine Mining Company in Harrison County.

NIGHTHAWKS: FAMILY CAPRIMULGIDAE

Common Nighthawk *Chordeiles minor*

The Common Nighthawk is a fairly common migrant and an uncommon summer resident in agricultural and urban habitats, primarily in the western half of the region. The first migrants arrive in late April. They remain in fall until October or early November. In the east where they are mostly absent in summer, they occur in spring until early June.

Chuck-will's-widow *Caprimulgus carolinensis*

Chuck-will's-widows are a fairly common summer resident in mature woodlands with a dense ground cover of leafy debris. They are absent from the Blackland Prairie except probably as migrants. In spring they are not detected until calling begins in early or mid-April. They are seldom heard after late August, though there are records until early October.

Whip-poor-will *Caprimulgus vociferus*

The Whip-poor-will is an uncommon spring migrant, especially in eastern areas of the region; in the west it is rare and irregular. Its status in fall is poorly known. The first spring migrants are detected between late March and late May, when they call for about five minutes just after dusk and then again just before dawn. Fall migrants are silent, making their status difficult to assess. They are thought to occur from late August through early October.

SWIFTS: FAMILY APODIDAE

Chimney Swift *Chaetura pelagica*

Chimney Swifts are common summer residents throughout the region. They nest in chimneys and are found around towns and farmhouses. In spring the first birds arrive in March, and they remain through October or early November.

HUMMINGBIRDS: FAMILY TROCHILIDAE

Green Violet-ear *Colibri thalassinus*

The Green Violet-ear is an accidental summer visitor. One was photographed at a feeder in Henderson, in Rusk County, from June 13 to 17, 1997 (TBRC 1997-113).

Ruby-throated Hummingbird *Archilochus colubris*

The Ruby-throated Hummingbird is a fairly common migrant and summer resident. The first arrivals are usually in March. They remain until October.

Black-chinned Hummingbird *Archilochus alexandri*

The Black-chinned Hummingbird is possibly a rare migrant in Northeast Texas. The only record for the region is one given without details by Pulich (1988) for Hunt County. Females and immature birds of this species are very similar to the Ruby-throated Hummingbirds and are easy to overlook.

Anna's Hummingbird *Calypte anna*

The Anna's Hummingbird is a very rare fall and winter visitor. The only records involve an adult male that visited a feeder near Daingerfield, in Morris County, from early December, 1995, through February 4, 1996, and an immature male that put in appearances over two days at a Longview feeder from September 22 to 24, 1999.

Calliope Hummingbird *Stellula calliope*

The Calliope Hummingbird is a very rare migrant in Northeast Texas. The only record for the region involves a bird that was photographed feeding on Turk's cap in a residential yard in Commerce, in Hunt County, on October 25, 2000. As is the case for several other species of western hummingbirds, a few Calliope Hummingbirds have been wintering in the southeastern United States in recent years.

Broad-tailed Hummingbird *Selasphorus platycercus*

The Broad-tailed Hummingbird is a very rare migrant and winter visitor in Northeast Texas. A bird remained at a feeder in Kilgore, in Rusk County, from November 12, 1998, through April 4, 1999. Oberholser (1974) cites a fall record for Harrison County without details.

Rufous Hummingbird *Selasphorus rufus*

The Rufous Hummingbird is probably a rare visitor from late summer through midwinter. Females and immatures of this genus, which includes the Rufous, Allen's, and Broad-tailed hummingbirds, are extremely difficult—often impossible—to identify with certainty. Rufous Hummingbirds are increasingly noted in eastern North America, and there are about a dozen records of birds thought to be this species in Northeast Texas.

Allen's Hummingbird *Selasphorus sasin*

The Allen's Hummingbird is an accidental visitor. Hummingbird expert Nancy Newfield of Louisiana identified as this species a bird found dead below a hummingbird feeder in Canton, in Van Zandt County, on January 1, 1995. The bird had been present since early December, 1994.

KINGFISHERS: FAMILY ALCEDINIDAE

Belted Kingfisher *Ceryle alcyon*

Belted Kingfishers are fairly common permanent residents around ponds, lakes, streams, and seasonally flooded fields. They nest in sandy banks, usually adjacent to water. They often sit on dead limbs or utility wires over water.

WOODPECKERS: FAMILY PICIDAE

Red-headed Woodpecker *Melanerpes erythrocephalus*

The Red-headed Woodpecker is a locally uncommon to rare summer resident in forested parts of the region. It is also an uncommon to rare migrant and winter resident throughout the area. During summer these woodpeckers occur locally where dead trees are available, from upland woodlands to sloughs and wetlands in the bottomland hardwood forests, and in the standing dead timber of area lakes. Fall migrants are quite evident, especially in western areas during September and October, when several dozen per day can often be seen migrating south—generally at low altitudes, often just over the treetops, and frequently with migrating Northern Flickers. There is no evidence of a similar phenomenon in spring; however, most of the nonbreeding population departs by early May.

Red-bellied Woodpecker *Melanerpes carolinus*

Red-bellied Woodpeckers are common permanent residents throughout the region. They are not known be migratory, although several potential migrants were recorded in early October, 1998, flying around Cooper Lake with a large number of migrant Northern Flickers.

Yellow-bellied Sapsucker *Sphyrapicus varius*

The Yellow-bellied Sapsucker is a fairly common winter resident. The first fall migrants arrive in late September, although most do not arrive until the first or second week of October. Generally they remain until March, and there are few records in early April.

Downy Woodpecker *Picoides pubescens*

The Downy Woodpecker is a common permanent resident in all types of woodland and scrubby habitats throughout the region.

Hairy Woodpecker *Picoides villosus*

The Hairy Woodpecker is an uncommon to rare localized summer resident in mature woodlands, primarily in the eastern sections of the region. With an influx of wintering birds, the species is somewhat more common in fall and winter throughout the region. It is interesting that during these seasons Hairy Woodpeckers are often found in open areas on the Blackland Prairie and in scattered or isolated trees along fences and in pastures. It is not clear when the first fall migrants begin to arrive; one at Big Creek Lake (where the species does not nest) on October 16, 1998, may have been an early migrant. Similarly, it is not known when they migrate north again in spring, though most are gone by March or April.

Northern Flicker *Colaptes auratus*

The "Yellow-shafted" race of the Northern Flicker is a common migrant and winter resident. The birds breed in mature forests along the Red River and generally east of a line from Paris to Winnsboro and Tyler. The first fall migrants are recorded in September, sometimes in the early part of the month but often not until much later. During early October migration can be spectacular, especially at local lakes: following cool fronts, dozens of birds per hour may be recorded skirting the lakes to avoid flying over the water. They remain common winter residents, possibly more common in some years than others, until about mid-March, when they begin to disappear quietly. The last are noted in early April. The "Red-shafted" Flicker, *C. a. cafer,* is an uncommon to rare migrant and winter resident.

Pileated Woodpecker *Dryocopus pileatus*

The Pileated Woodpecker is an uncommon to fairly common resident in heavily wooded country in the east and a rare, localized, permanent resident in the mature bottomland hardwood forests along the larger creeks and rivers in the west.

FLYCATCHERS: FAMILY TYRANNIDAE

Olive-sided Flycatcher *Contopus cooperi*

The Olive-sided Flycatcher is an uncommon migrant. During migration individuals almost always select the very top of a dead tree, usually one that affords a panoramic view of the surrounding trees, from which to hawk insects. They are recorded in fall from early August through late September or early October and in spring from mid- to late April through late May.

Eastern Wood-Pewee *Contopus virens*

Eastern Wood-Pewees are fairly common summer residents and migrants in open woodlands, often with little or no understory vegetation. They are generally absent as breeders on the Blackland Prairie. The first spring migrants or summer residents appear in late April or early May. Singing begins shortly thereafter and continues until about early August. The last migrants are noted in late September or early October.

Yellow-bellied Flycatcher *Empidonax flaviventris*

The Yellow-bellied Flycatcher is a rare migrant throughout the region. Spring sightings range from late April through late May while in fall the species is recorded from mid- to late September.

Acadian Flycatcher *Empidonax virescens*

The Acadian Flycatcher is an uncommon summer resident in extensive areas of moist, mature woodlands and seasonally flooded swamps. The species is generally absent on the Blackland Prairie, except in large forested areas along rivers or bigger creeks. The first migrants are not detected until singing begins in mid- to late April. They probably remain until late August or early September, but identification of nonsinging birds is difficult.

Alder Flycatcher *Empidonax alnorum;* **Willow Flycatcher** *Empidonax traillii*

Members of the "Traill's" Flycatcher complex, which includes the Willow and Alder flycatchers, are fairly common migrants. These similar species were only recently determined to be separate species and are difficult to identify. Little reliable information is available about the migratory status of each, especially in fall when they seldom sing. Members of this complex are recorded from mid-April through late May and from mid-August to mid- or late October.

Least Flycatcher *Empidonax minimus*
The Least Flycatcher is a fairly common migrant. This small size and characteristic *whit* call of this empidonax make it one of the easiest of this genus to identify. These flycatchers occur in spring from mid-April into early June and in fall from late July through October.

Black Phoebe *Sayornis nigricans*
There is one report of a Black Phoebe on White Oak Creek in Titus County on November 8, 1976. Although this one was an unlikely stray, there are four records from nearby north-central Texas.

Eastern Phoebe *Sayornis phoebe*
The Eastern Phoebe is a fairly common migrant and an uncommon summer and winter resident throughout Northeast Texas. Eastern Phoebes become slightly more common in September and October and again in March and April, perhaps reflecting an influx of migrants through the region. They often nest around homes or under porches, in barns, and under bridges.

Say's Phoebe *Sayornis saya*
The Say's Phoebe is a rare migrant and winter visitor. There are seven records, including one at Big Creek Lake on November 17, 1990, one at Longview on January 3, 1993, and another at Lake O' the Pines on September 21, 1993. One was photographed near a residence at Gough, in Delta County, on March 2, 2000. Another was near Cooper Lake on April 6, 2000. One remained near the

Sabine Mining Company, in Harrison County, from October 22, 2000 to March 5, 2001. Finally, one was present at Cooper Lake from October 24 to January, 2001.

Vermilion Flycatcher *Pyrocephalus rubinus*
The Vermilion Flycatcher is a rare fall migrant and winter visitor. There are over a dozen recent records ranging from late September through early March from all parts of Northeast Texas. The species often occurs around willow-lined lakes and ponds.

Ash-throated Flycatcher *Myiarchus cinerascens*
The Ash-throated Flycatcher is a very rare spring or even accidental migrant in Northeast Texas. There is a single sight record from near Caddo Lake on May 11, 1996.

Great Crested Flycatcher *Myiarchus crinitus*
Great Crested Flycatchers are fairly common summer residents in a variety of woodlands, including urban areas. They occur from late March through early October.

Western Kingbird *Tyrannus verticalis*
Western Kingbirds are fairly common summer residents in urban areas and around rural houses where the grass is kept mowed. They are most common in the western sections of the region, though recently they have expanded eastward, now occurring locally throughout all of Northeast Texas. These birds favor utility wires almost exclusively and often build their nests on power poles, especially between the transformer and the pole. The first spring arrivals are noted on the breeding grounds in late April. Summer residents are conspicuous in urban areas until late July or early August, when they suddenly disappear. A few migrants from elsewhere continue to trickle through until September. The summer range of the Western Kingbird has moved steadily eastward in Texas, primarily in urban areas, during the past hundred years.

Eastern Kingbird *Tyrannus tyrannus*

The Eastern Kingbird is a common migrant and an uncommon summer resident. A few spring migrants begin appearing in early April, and they become common later in the month. Most have departed by mid-September although a few are seen in late September or early October.

Scissor-tailed Flycatcher *Tyrannus forficatus*

The Scissor-tailed Flycatcher is a common migrant and fairly common summer resident in a variety of open habitats throughout the region. A few migrants (usually males with long tails) are sometimes found during the middle of March, although large numbers do not arrive until early April. During summer they are widespread in open habitats, such as cattle pastures with scattered trees, around farms and rural houses, and near parking lots and some urban areas. They often hunt from utility wires and most often build their nests in trees or shrubs. During late summer and early fall, several dozen are often found staging along utility wires in rural and urban areas. They become harder to find as the weather grows cooler in late October, although they have been known to linger until November or December.

SHRIKES: FAMILY LANIIDAE

Loggerhead Shrike *Lanius ludovicianus*

Loggerhead Shrikes are fairly common winter residents and uncommon to rare breeding residents. They prefer wide open areas, such as agricultural fields, and are frequently seen perched on barbed wire fences and telephone wires as well as on small trees and shrubs. Although the local breeding population seems to have declined in recent years, the species is still fairly common in fall and winter. Nesting begins by mid-March, when most of the wintering birds begin to depart. Fall migrants begin arriving in early or mid-August and these shrikes are once again fairly common by late September.

VIREOS: FAMILY VIREONIDAE

White-eyed Vireo *Vireo griseus*

The White-eyed Vireo is a common summer resident in moist and dense secondary growth and early succession habitats. Territorial birds begin singing from dense vegetation in early or mid-March. Most have departed by October, although there are a few records into December from scattered locations.

Bell's Vireo *Vireo bellii*

The Bell's Vireo is a rare migrant and very local summer resident throughout most of the region except on the Blackland Prairie, where it is a locally uncommon breeding species. During summer these vireos occur in dense thickets and fencerows and in willows beside ponds and creeks. Most are detected only on the breeding grounds, which are usually occupied by late April or early May. Little is known about fall migration; there are a few records away from the breeding grounds in August and early September that are likely migrants.

Yellow-throated Vireo *Vireo flavifrons*

Yellow-throated Vireos are fairly common summer residents in the forested eastern half of the region and rare migrants in the western half. They arrive on territory in mid- to late March and remain there until late September or early October. There are few records of migrants away from the breeding grounds.

Blue-headed Vireo *Vireo solitarius*

The Blue-headed Vireo is an uncommon migrant and a rare to uncommon winter resident. Fall migrants typically occur from September through November, though a few individuals can be always found in the region during the winter months—especially in the southern counties. The onset of spring migration is perhaps masked by the presence of wintering individuals but likely extends from early April through late May.

Warbling Vireo *Vireo gilvus*

The Warbling Vireo is an uncommon migrant throughout Northeast Texas. It is a very rare summer visitor. Spring migrants are normally noted from mid-April through late May. Fall migration is mainly from late August through late September, though there is a record of an exceptionally early fall migrant from Cooper Lake on August 7, 1998. In *The Bird Life of Texas* Oberholser lists summer records for Marion and Harrison counties. In 1988 a singing bird was found in midsummer near Tyler. Warbling Vireos only occasionally breed in Texas.

Philadelphia Vireo *Vireo philadelphicus*

The Philadelphia Vireo is a rare to uncommon spring migrant and a very rare fall migrant. Spring migrants are noted from mid-April to late May. There are few records for fall—mainly in September—and the status of the species at that season is poorly known.

Red-eyed Vireo *Vireo olivaceus*

Red-eyed Vireos are common summer residents in mature woodlands mainly in the eastern sections of the region. In the Blackland Prairie and Post Oak Savannah they are uncommon summer residents, largely along rivers and bigger creeks. They occur from late March and early April through October.

JAYS AND CROWS: FAMILY CORVIDAE

Blue Jay *Cyanocitta cristata*

Blue Jays are fairly common permanent residents and common to abundant migrants. Flocks of Blue Jays, some of the groups quite large, begin migrating into the region from mid- to late September. Then during the first two weeks of October several hundred per hour are frequently noted flying south in loose strings, often just a few feet above the treetops. Beginning in mid-April, a similar phenomenon is noted with birds flying north, although the peak is much shorter and the flocks are typically not as large. They are probably still moving north by early May, although it is not clear just how long spring migration lasts.

American Crow *Corvus brachyrhynchos*

The American Crow is a common permanent resident in a wide variety of habitats throughout the region.

Fish Crow *Corvus ossifragus*

The Fish Crow is a fairly common permanent resident in Bowie and Cass counties south to Caddo Lake. Following a dramatic range expansion in the past several decades, the range of the species extends west in summer along the Red River to Fannin County and along the Sulphur River to Cooper Lake (White 2000). Fish Crows have occurred as vagrants at Lake Fork Reservoir and Lake Tawakoni.

LARKS: FAMILY ALAUDIDAE

Horned Lark *Eremophila alpestris*

The Horned Lark is a fairly common winter resident in large plowed or fallow fields. In summer it is an uncommon and local nesting species, most frequently in large cotton fields on the Blackland Prairie and Post Oak Savannah. In winter these larks usually occur in large flocks and forage over plowed fields with Lapland Longspurs, although it is not uncommon to find them in cattle pastures or parking lots or along lakeshores.

SWALLOWS: FAMILY HIRUNDINIDAE

Purple Martin *Progne subis*

The Purple Martin is a fairly common to uncommon summer resident in urban areas and around farmhouses where martin houses are maintained. The first scouts arrive in late January or February, followed by larger numbers in March and April. By late June or early July the birds depart to area lakes to form large premigratory roosts. They are largely gone by mid-September, though an occasional bird is seen in early October.

Tree Swallow *Tachycineta bicolor*

The Tree Swallow is an uncommon migrant and localized summer breeding resident in Northeast Texas. Since 1991 several pairs have nested at Big Creek Lake and Lake Fork Reservoir. Since

1994 small numbers also have been noted near the standing dead timber in Cooper Lake. A few juvenile birds were discovered there in the summer of 1998. In 1999 around one hundred pairs bred there, and an additional breeding pair was located at the Texas Eastman Chemical Plant near Longview. Tree Swallows nest in woodpecker cavities or nest boxes in the flooded timber. They are among the first swallows to arrive in the spring, often appearing on breeding territory by late February or early March. Elsewhere, migrants are noted passing through during March and April with a few still moving through in May. Fall migration extends from mid-July through November, with a few individuals occasionally lingering into mid-December.

Northern Rough-winged Swallow *Stelgidopteryx serripennis*
Northern Rough-winged Swallows are fairly common migrants and uncommon localized breeding residents. They nest in tunnels burrowed out of sandy banks, often near water. The first spring migrants are often single birds in late February. They become more common in March and continue passing through until May. Fall migrants are difficult to distinguish from summering birds but probably begin to arrive in July or August, with some continuing through November or even December.

Bank Swallow *Riparia riparia*
The Bank Swallow is an uncommon to rare spring migrant, a fairly common to uncommon fall migrant, and a very rare summer visitor. It occurs in spring from late April through late May. There are a couple of summer records from Delta County. No evidence of breeding exists, though it is possible that this species has nested in the banks of the North Sulphur River channel along the northern boundary of Delta County. Surveys should be conducted in summer to determine if individuals are present or breeding. Fall migration is from mid-July and August through late September or October.

Cliff Swallow *Petrochelidon pyrrhonota*

The Cliff Swallow is a fairly common migrant and localized breeding resident under overpasses and bridges. This colonial species has been expanding its breeding range eastward through Northeast Texas in recent years. The first migrants appear in March and begin nesting soon after that. After breeding is complete, large flocks often form around the larger lakes in the region, where they remain until October or November.

Cave Swallow *Petrochelidon fulva*

The Cave Swallow is a rare spring and summer visitor to the western counties of Northeast Texas. This rapidly expanding species was first recorded in the region on September 1, 1995, at Cooper Lake, presumably as a post-breeding visitor. In 1999 several Cave Swallow nests were found in Cliff Swallow colonies in Hopkins and Delta counties. Additional sightings have come from a Cliff Swallow colony below the spillway at Lake Tawakoni, in Rains and Van Zandt counties. Recent summer records from Hunt County are also suggestive of nesting, though no nest sites have been found. Sightings range from late May through early September.

Barn Swallow *Hirundo rustica*

The Barn Swallow is an abundant migrant and a common summer resident. Barn Swallows breed in a variety of areas, including culverts, barns, eaves of porches and awnings, garages, and similar areas. The first few sightings are in late February and early March. The birds remain all summer and begin to depart in October and November, a few often lingering until December during mild years.

TITMICE AND CHICKADEES: FAMILY PARIDAE

Carolina Chickadee *Poecile carolinensis*

The Carolina Chickadee is a common permanent resident in the area. This species is widespread and occurs almost anywhere that trees and shrubby or brushy vegetation are present.

Tufted Titmouse *Baeolophus bicolor*

The Tufted Titmouse is a fairly common to locally uncommon permanent resident—decidedly less common than the related Carolina Chickadee.

NUTHATCHES: FAMILY SITTIDAE

Red-breasted Nuthatch *Sitta canadensis*

The Red-breasted Nuthatch is an irregular migrant and winter resident in the region, often more common in the Pineywoods than elsewhere. Every few years this species stages larger than usual "invasions" south of the breeding grounds in the northern forests. During these years it is not uncommon to find these birds in all types of habitats. Most of the records have been during years when they invade into the region.

White-breasted Nuthatch *Sitta carolinensis*

The White-breasted Nuthatch is an uncommon resident in mature post oak woodlands and mature riparian woodlands in the Post Oak Savannah and locally rare in the Pineywoods. It is generally absent on the Blackland Prairie, except possibly as a rare winter migrant from the north.

Brown-headed Nuthatch *Sitta pusilla*

The Brown-headed Nuthatch is a fairly common permanent resident in the pine and pine-oak woodland in the eastern half of the region.

CREEPERS: FAMILY CERTHIIDAE

Brown Creeper *Certhia americana*

The Brown Creeper is an uncommon to fairly common winter resident. The first fall migrants are usually not detected until late October or November (or even later), although they have occurred by the middle of October. The birds are normally present until March. Although Brown Creepers are usually fairly common, they are somewhat irregular in occurrence. In some years they are widespread and found in a variety of habitats, but in other years they are generally restricted to mature woodlands.

WRENS: FAMILY TROGLODYTIDAE

Rock Wren *Salpinctes obsoletus*

The Rock Wren is a rare visitor to Northeast Texas during fall and winter. Individuals typically occur along the rock-covered impoundments of the area reservoirs. There are about ten records ranging from late September through late February.

Carolina Wren *Thryothorus ludovicianus*

Carolina Wrens are common permanent residents in a variety of woodland and urban habitats throughout the region. They are often found nesting around homes and in garages, barns, tool sheds, and similar settings.

Bewick's Wren *Thryomanes bewickii*

The Bewick's Wren is an uncommon migrant and winter resident in a variety of brushy habitats in the Post Oak Savannah and Blackland Prairie and is rare and very local in heavily wooded areas. These wrens occur in brushy fencerows adjacent to open areas and also around houses, in yards, and along wooden fences and log piles. Fall migrants and winter residents are sometimes noted in mid- to late September, becoming more common in early October. They remain until early to mid-March, rarely until mid-April. At least three races are known to occur. The dull reddish-backed and gray-breasted birds from the eastern United States, *T. b. bewickii,* which have suffered massive declines in eastern North American in recent years, are uncommon to rare. The recently described *T. b. pulichi* from northern Oklahoma and Kansas, which is very similar to *bewickii* but brighter reddish on the back and brighter white on the breast (Phillips 1986; Pyle 1997), is a fairly common migrant and winter resident. Some of the migrants and winter residents are also the brown-backed, gray-breasted *T. b. cryptus,* which nests in Texas and portions of Oklahoma, west to Grayson and Dallas counties and south into Central Texas. The timing, distribution, and habitats of the races are still being studied. It appears that *pulichi* is the latest to migrate in spring—singing individuals have been noted until mid-April. None of these races is known to nest in the area.

House Wren *Troglodytes aedon*

The House Wren is a fairly common migrant and an uncommon winter resident. Fall migration stretches from early September through November. These wrens have increased in recent years during the winter months and are now regular in brushy second growth and scrub habitats throughout the region. Spring migration probably begins in April and lasts until late May. There is one sight record of the western race, *T. a. parkmanii,* from Big Creek Lake on October 26, 1997.

Winter Wren *Troglodytes troglodytes*

Winter Wrens are fairly common to uncommon winter residents in mature woods and along streams and wooded lakeshores. They arrive in early October and remain until late March or early April.

Sedge Wren *Cistothorus platensis*

The Sedge Wren is an uncommon to locally common migrant and winter resident and a very rare and localized summer visitor. Fall migrants usually arrive in small numbers in mid- to late September—though they have arrived by early August—becoming numerous in October and remaining until April, with a few still present in late May. There are at least three summer records in August, including two recent ones at Cooper Lake and an old record from Harrison County. In late August of 1995 three pairs arrived in a large grassy pasture near Cooper Lake and began singing and defending territories. During wet summers, Sedge Wrens often move a bit southward and sometimes attempt to breed (Bedell 1996). One in smartweed at the upper end of Cooper Lake on August 9, 1997, provides the earliest fall record for the area.

Marsh Wren *Cistothorus palustris*
The Marsh Wren is a locally uncommon to rare migrant and winter resident in cattail marshes and very rarely in wet grassy fields and grassy lakeshores in the region. The first fall migrants usually appear by late September or early October, although a few have arrived by early September. In winter small numbers are found in appropriate habitat. Spring migration begins in April and stretches into mid- or late May.

KINGLETS: FAMILY REGULIDAE

Golden-crowned Kinglet *Regulus satrapa*
The Golden-crowned Kinglet is an uncommon to fairly common winter resident. This species is quite variable in abundance from year to year. Some years the birds are quite numerous and are present in a variety of brushy and wooded habitats, while in other years they are much less common, or even irregular in occurrence, and confined to mature woodlands. The timing of fall migration often coincides with that of the Brown Creeper. During years in which Golden-crowned Kinglets are more common, they often arrive in the middle of the second week of October, although frequently the first arrivals are not noted until late October or early November. They remain until late March or early April.

Ruby-crowned Kinglet *Regulus calendula*
The Ruby-crowned Kinglet is a common migrant and winter resident. The first fall migrants usually arrive in early to mid-September and they regularly remain in spring until April, with a few birds occasionally lingering until mid-May.

GNATCATCHERS: FAMILY SYLVIIDAE

Blue-gray Gnatcatcher *Polioptila caerulea*
Blue-gray Gnatcatchers are fairly common migrants and summer residents and uncommon winter residents in Northeast Texas. They are largely absent in summer from many parts of the Blackland Prairie except in moist wooded areas along rivers and large creeks. There are records for all months of the year, though there is an

influx of fall migrants from September through November and a spring influx from March through May.

THRUSHES: FAMILY TURDIDAE

Eastern Bluebird *Sialia sialis*

Eastern Bluebirds are fairly common breeding residents around houses and barns, along roadsides, and in similar open areas in the Post Oak Savannah and the Pineywoods. They are uncommon to rare in parts of the Blackland Prairie where there are few trees, except in winter, when there is often an influx of migrants from the north.

Mountain Bluebird *Sialia currucoides*

The Mountain Bluebird is a very rare winter visitor in Northeast Texas. In *The Birds of North Central Texas* Pulich (1988) indicates records for Hunt and Fannin counties. The Hunt record is likely based on an old report from the Commerce area in February and March, 1940.

Townsend's Solitaire *Myadestes townsendi*

The Townsend's Solitaire is a very rare visitor in Northeast Texas. There are two reports of this western species: one is listed by Pulich (1988) for Hunt County on March 14, 1948, and more recently one was reported from Fannin County in the spring of 1997.

Veery *Catharus fuscescens*

The Veery is a rare to uncommon spring migrant throughout the region. There are no fall records. Spring sightings range from late April through mid-May.

Gray-cheeked Thrush *Catharus minimus*

The Gray-cheeked Thrush is a rare to uncommon spring migrant and possibly a very rare fall migrant. There are spring records from mid-April through late May. Its status in fall is uncertain, though there are apparently one or two sight records at this season from the eastern sections of the region.

Swainson's Thrush *Catharus ustulatus*

The Swainson's Thrush is a common spring migrant in moist woodlands throughout the region and a rare fall migrant, primarily in the forested eastern sections. Dense concentrations of migrants are often found in early May near fruiting mulberry trees. Spring migration typically begins in mid-April, though there is an early record of two birds in Hunt County on March 14, 1992. Spring migration often continues through late May and even into early June. Fall records are in September and October.

Hermit Thrush *Catharus guttatus*

The Hermit Thrush is an uncommon winter resident from October through March. It prefers dense thickets, or mature woodlands with a leafy understory, often in the vicinity of an eastern red cedar.

Wood Thrush *Hylocichla mustelina*

The Wood Thrush is an uncommon to fairly common breeding resident in heavily forested tracts in the eastern half of the region. Individuals arrive in mid- to late March and remain through September or October. Elsewhere, the species is a rare migrant.

American Robin *Turdus migratorius*

American Robins are common winter residents and migrants. They are fairly common summer residents locally in urban areas. During winter massive concentrations are frequently observed at evening roosts, often in dense thickets of eastern red cedar.

MOCKINGBIRDS AND THRASHERS: FAMILY MIMIDAE

Gray Catbird *Dumatella carolinensis*

The Gray Catbird is an uncommon to fairly common migrant and a rare, localized summer resident, primarily in urban areas. The species is a rare winter visitor, mainly in the southeastern part of the region. During spring migration small concentrations are often noted feeding on mulberries. Fall migration probably stretches from early September through early October, though there are a few records from Christmas Bird Counts in the southeastern part of the region.

The first spring migrants appear in late March or early April, numbers not peaking until late April or early May. Most have departed by late May, although there are several scattered summer records.

Northern Mockingbird *Mimus polyglottos*
The Northern Mockingbird is a common permanent resident in a variety of habitats throughout the region.

Sage Thrasher *Oreoscoptes montanus*
The Sage Thrasher is a very rare winter visitor in Northeast Texas. There are four regional records: one in Commerce from December 2, 1956, through February 10, 1957; one in Greenville on January 3, 1981; one near Lake O' the Pines in Ore City, in Marion County, on November 6, 1994; and one at Texas Eastman Chemical Plant near Longview on October 19, 1997.

Brown Thrasher *Toxostoma rufum*
The Brown Thrasher is a common migrant and winter resident and an uncommon summer resident in urban areas. There is a noticeable influx in September of migrants, presumably from farther north. The birds remain common all winter but begin to disappear from many areas by March, although they breed in many cities and towns throughout the region and occasionally in dense tangles in undeveloped rural areas.

Curve-billed Thrasher *Toxostoma curvirostre*
The Curve-billed Thrasher is an accidental visitor in Northeast Texas. One was photographed near the Sabine River Authority Office at Lake Tawakoni, in Rains County, during its stay from December 18, 1992, through January 3, 1993.

STARLINGS: FAMILY STURNIDAE

European Starling *Sturnus vulgaris*
The European Starling is a common permanent resident and an abundant migrant and winter resident. In winter large numbers of

starlings, blackbirds, grackles, and cowbirds form huge flocks that roam the countryside.

PIPITS: FAMILY MOTACILLIDAE

American Pipit *Anthus rubescens*

The American Pipit is a fairly common migrant and winter resident. It occurs from late September through April in large areas of short grass or in plowed fields, along lake shores, and on the rocky impoundments of area lakes.

Sprague's Pipit *Anthus spragueii*

Sprague's Pipits are locally uncommon but regular migrants and winter residents. They occur mainly in the Blackland Prairie and Post Oak Savannah and are probably rare and irregular in suitable habitat farther east. They are most common at Lake Tawakoni, where they occur from early October through early April.

WAXWINGS: FAMILY BOMBYCILLIDAE

Bohemian Waxwing *Bombycilla garrulus*

The Bohemian Waxwing is an accidental winter visitor. One was documented in a flock of Cedar Waxwings at Cooper Lake, in Hopkins County, on February 26, 2000 (TBRC 2000-37).

Cedar Waxwing *Bombycilla cedrorum*

Cedar Waxwings are fairly common winter residents. They arrive late in the fall, usually not until late November or early December, and they remain late in spring, sometimes until late May or early June.

WOOD WARBLERS: FAMILY PARULIDAE

Blue-winged Warbler *Vermivora pinus*

The Blue-winged Warbler is a rare to uncommon migrant in the area, with records in spring from mid-April through mid-May and in fall from early to late September, rarely into late October.

Golden-winged Warbler *Vermivora chrysoptera*

The Golden-winged Warbler is a rare spring migrant and a very rare fall migrant. Spring records are from late April through mid-May. There are a few fall records from mid-September and a very late report from Lake Fork Reservoir on November 28, 1990.

Tennessee Warbler *Vermivora peregrina*

The Tennessee Warbler is a common spring and an uncommon fall migrant. During spring migration, which stretches from late April through early June, this is one of the most common warblers in the region. Fall migrants occur from early August through early October.

Orange-crowned Warbler *Vermivora celata*

The Orange-crowned Warbler is a fairly common migrant and winter resident. It arrives in late September or early October and remains until mid-May. Orange-crowned Warblers are especially fond of dense tangles of vines, trees, or scrub, especially eastern red cedar thickets that retain green leaves all winter. The nominate eastern race *V. c. celata* is the normal migrant and winter resident in the region. A bright yellow individual thought to be the "Rocky Mountain" Orange-crowned Warbler, *V. c. orestera,* was studied on April 2, 1996, at Cooper Lake.

Nashville Warbler *Vermivora ruficapilla*

The Nashville Warbler is a common migrant in the western half of the region and uncommon to rare in the east. It is very rare in mid-winter. On the Blackland Prairie and Post Oak Savannah this species is one of the most conspicuous warblers during migration, especially in fall. Spring records are from mid-March through late May, while fall records are from late August through mid-November. There are a couple of recent records from area Christmas Bird Counts.

Northern Parula *Parula americana*

The Northern Parula is a common nesting species in wet swampy woods and bottomland hardwood forests in the forested eastern half of the region. Elsewhere, especially in the Blackland Prairie, the birds are local summer residents along several of the larger rivers and tributary creeks. They occur from early March through late October. Away from the breeding grounds they occur as rare to uncommon migrants, primarily in April and May and from late August through late October.

Yellow Warbler *Dendroica petechia*

The Yellow Warbler is a common spring and fall migrant. It is very rare in midsummer and is not known to nest in Northeast Texas. Yellow Warblers are usually the most abundant migrant warblers in the region. This is one of the latest warblers to arrive in spring and the earliest to return in the fall. Spring migrants occur from late April though late May or early June, and fall migrants occur from late July to early October. Oberholser (1974) cites summer records for several counties.

Chestnut-sided Warbler *Dendroica penslyvanica*

Chestnut-sided Warblers are uncommon spring migrants and very rare fall migrants. They occur in spring from late April through late May. The only fall records suggest that they occur from about early to late September, although records in October are likely.

Magnolia Warbler *Dendroica magnolia*

The Magnolia Warbler is a fairly common spring migrant and a rare fall migrant in Northeast Texas. It may be a very rare winter visitor. Spring migration is from mid-April through late May. There are fewer than a dozen fall records, ranging from early September through late October. There is one winter report for the Caddo Lake area in the mid-1960s.

Cape May Warbler *Dendroica tigrina*

The Cape May Warbler is a very rare spring migrant in Northeast Texas. It occurs mainly in late April or early May, though there are fewer than a half dozen records. Although there are no fall or winter records from the region, this warbler should be watched for in those seasons among flocks of Yellow-rumped Warblers.

Black-throated Blue Warbler *Dendroica caerulescens*
The Black-throated Blue Warbler is a very rare spring migrant. There are only a handful of regional records—all from early to mid-May. Most have been from the eastern sections of the region.

Yellow-rumped Warbler *Dendroica coronata*
The Yellow-rumped Warbler is an abundant migrant and winter resident in a wide variety of habitats throughout the region. Most are the eastern "Myrtle" Warbler, formerly considered a distinct species. The western "Audubon's" Warbler has been recorded on several occasions. Small numbers of Yellow-rumped Warblers begin arriving in mid-October. They become common by the end of the month and remain common until mid-April. A few have been recorded until early or mid-May.

Black-throated Green Warbler *Dendroica virens*
The Black-throated Green Warbler is a fairly common migrant throughout the region. Spring records are from early April through late May, while fall records range from early August through mid-October.

Blackburnian Warbler *Dendroica fusca*
The Blackburnian Warbler is an uncommon spring migrant from late April through late May. It is a very rare fall migrant and has been recorded only a few times, mainly in early October.

Yellow-throated Warbler *Dendroica dominica*
Yellow-throated Warblers are fairly common breeding residents in upland pine or pine-oak woodlands and wet swampy bottomland hardwood forests in the eastern sections of the region. They occur from early March through late October. In the west they are rare migrants, mainly during April, May, September, and October.

Pine Warbler *Dendroica pinus*
The Pine Warbler is a common breeding species in the Pineywoods of Northeast Texas. It also occurs locally in stands of pines or pine-

oak woodlands in parts of the Post Oak Savannah. Elsewhere it is a rare to uncommon migrant and winter resident—generally from late October through late April or early May.

Prairie Warbler *Dendroica discolor*

Prairie Warblers are fairly common breeding residents in brushy habitats—such as clear-cuts and pine plantations—in the eastern portions of the region. They occur from early April through late September. Elsewhere they are rare, but possibly regular, migrants in late April and early May and again from early August through mid-September. There are two recent midwinter records of this rare winter visitor, one at Lake Tawakoni from December 6 to 12, 1995, and another at Camp Tyler on January 5, 1996.

Palm Warbler *Dendroica palmarum*

The Palm Warbler is a rare migrant, and a very rare winter visitor, in Northeast Texas. It occurs in spring from late April to late May and in fall from mid-September through October or November, and there are a couple of winter records. Most records are thought to have involved the western race, *D. p. palmarum*. The only record of the eastern race, *D. p. hypochrysea,* the "Yellow" Palm Warbler, was an individual at Cooper Lake on September 28, 2000.

Bay-breasted Warbler *Dendroica castanea*

The Bay-breasted Warbler is a rare spring migrant and a very rare fall migrant and winter visitor. It occurs in spring from late April through late May. Singles seen in Rusk County on September 4, 1992, and at Lake Tawakoni in September, 2000, provide the only fall reports for the region. This species has occasionally lingered until early winter across parts of North America, and there is well-documented sight record for Gregg County on January 1, 1994.

Blackpoll Warbler *Dendroica striata*

Blackpoll Warblers are rare to uncommon spring migrants in the region. They occur from late April through mid-May. There are no documented fall records in the region.

Cerulean Warbler *Dendroica cerulea*

The Cerulean Warbler is a very rare spring migrant. There are several old summer records from Bowie County and a recent one for Camp County. Although most field guides include the northeastern tip of the region within the summer range of the Cerulean Warbler, there is no recent evidence to suggest that they continue to nest here. A pair of birds was observed in midsummer of 1985 near the community of Lone Star in Camp County, but nesting was not confirmed. Recent migrant records have been from late April through mid-May.

Black-and-white Warbler *Mniotilta varia*

The Black-and-white Warbler is a common spring and fall migrant in a variety of wooded habitats throughout the region. It is an uncommon breeding resident in large undisturbed woodlands, arriving in late February or early March and lingering in fall through late October, with individuals occasionally lingering into November or December.

American Redstart *Setophaga ruticilla*

The American Redstart is a fairly common migrant, and a very local nesting resident, in Northeast Texas. Small numbers breed in bottomland woods along the Sulphur and Sabine rivers in the extreme eastern portions of the area. Elsewhere the birds occur as migrants from late April through mid-May and from late August until early October.

Prothonotary Warbler *Protonotaria citrea*

Prothonotary Warblers are locally common nesting residents in wet swampy bottomland hardwood forests and around lakes and ponds where plenty of dead trees are available for nest cavities. They arrive in early to mid-April and remain until mid-October.

Worm-eating Warbler *Helmitheros vermivorus*

The Worm-eating Warbler is a very rare migrant and a very local breeding resident in Northeast Texas. There are fewer than a dozen records of this species in the region, although there is a recent report of breeding in Gregg County. In *The Bird Life of Texas* Oberholser (1974) cites breeding records for Bowie and Cass counties and a summer record for Smith County. Records of migrants are few. There is a spring record for Hunt County on April 15, 1976, and the few fall records range from early August through mid-September. Clearly more fieldwork is needed to determine this species' status in the region.

Swainson's Warbler *Limnothlypis swainsonii*

Swainson's Warblers are locally uncommon breeding residents in wet bottomland forests with a dense covering of undergrowth and giant cane in eastern Northeast Texas. They arrive on breeding territory from late March through early April. They have been recorded in the region until late September. Elsewhere they are very rare migrants—mainly in April and May and from August through late September.

Ovenbird *Seiurus aurocapillus*

The Ovenbird is an uncommon spring and a rare fall migrant. It is very rare in early winter. Spring records stretch from late April and through late May. There are few fall records, all in September, though there are several October records for nearby counties in north-central Texas. There are a couple of early winter sightings from local Christmas Bird Counts.

Northern Waterthrush *Seiurus noveboracensis*

The Northern Waterthrush is an uncommon spring and fall migrant, especially around the wooded margins of lakes adjacent to standing dead timber. The birds are particularly fond of the shoreline, where they are typically seen walking, and are sometimes found in the dead timber of the lake as well. They occur in spring from mid-April to late May and probably in fall from mid-August through late September, though there are few records.

Louisiana Waterthrush *Seiurus motacilla*
The Louisiana Waterthrush is a locally uncommon breeding resident and an uncommon migrant in Northeast Texas. This species apparently requires slow-moving wooded creeks for nesting. It is possible that this habitat requirement has been created only recently by the slow discharge of water from artificial reservoirs and lakes. Birds arrive early in spring, typically in late March or early April. Breeding is probably complete by June. Fall migrants are occasionally noted from mid- or late July into late August or early September.

Kentucky Warbler *Oporornis formosus*
The Kentucky Warbler is a fairly common, though localized, breeding species in Northeast Texas. The species prefers mature deciduous woodlands or secondary growth with dense undergrowth, often on sandy ridges adjacent to bottomlands. The first spring birds arrive on territory in early or mid-April and begin singing. They sing until late June or early July and have departed by mid-September.

Mourning Warbler *Oporornis philadelphia*
The Mourning Warbler is an uncommon migrant. In spring it occurs from mid- to late April through early June and in fall from late August through mid-October.

Common Yellowthroat *Geothlypis trichas*
Common Yellowthroats are fairly common migrants and summer residents in a variety of brushy, grassy, and marshy habitats. In winter they are local residents in cattail marshes and wet grassy fields. There are records for all months of the year, with an influx of spring migrants from early April through late May. Fall migrants are often numerous from late August through late October or early November. Common Yellowthroats breed in low-lying grassy or marshy areas as well as in dense second growth woodlands.

Hooded Warbler *Wilsonia citrina*
Hooded Warblers are fairly common breeding residents in dense woodlands in the eastern third of the region. They arrive on breeding grounds in late March and remain until late October. Elsewhere in the region, they are rare spring migrants from late March through mid-May. There are very few records suggestive of fall migration.

Wilson's Warbler *Wilsonia pusilla*
The Wilson's Warbler is a fairly common migrant in a variety of wooded habitats throughout the region. It is a rare early winter lingering visitor. There are records in spring from late April through early June and in fall from mid-August through mid-October, and a few records of birds lingering until area Christmas Bird Counts.

Canada Warbler *Wilsonia canadensis*
The Canada Warbler is an uncommon spring and a rare fall migrant. Spring migration stretches from late April through late May; the species seems most common from May 10 to 15. The few fall records suggest that fall migration ranges from late August through mid-September.

Yellow-breasted Chat *Icteria virens*
The Yellow-breasted Chat is a locally common breeding resident in old fields, clear-cuts, thickets, and similar habitats—primarily in the eastern half of the region. In the west it is even more uncommon and local. Elsewhere it is an uncommon to rare migrant. Birds arrive on breeding territory in early to mid-April and are usually gone by early October. Migrants occur from mid-April to late May and probably from August through October.

TANAGERS: FAMILY THRAUPIDAE

Summer Tanager *Piranga rubra*
Summer Tanagers are fairly common summer residents in mature upland pine or pine-oak woodlands in the eastern sections of the region. They arrive in mid- to late April and begin singing and

defending territory at once. They remain until late September and early October.

Scarlet Tanager *Piranga olivacea*
The Scarlet Tanager is a rare migrant and a very rare summer visitor. Most records are from the eastern sections of the region, where the species occurs in spring from early April to late May and in fall from late August through mid-September. There are a few summer records from the area in June or July, though no evidence of breeding has been found.

SPARROWS AND BUNTINGS: FAMILY EMBERIZIDAE

Green-tailed Towhee *Pipilo chlorurus*
The Green-tailed Towhee is a very rare winter visitor in Northeast Texas. The only records cited by Oberholser (1974) are for Harrison and Smith counties, without dates or details.

Spotted Towhee *Pipilo maculatus*
The Spotted Towhee is a fairly common winter resident in brushy fields, second growth habitat, and open woodlands in the western counties of the region. It appears to be rare in the east, though more information is clearly needed concerning the status and distribution of this and the Eastern Towhee. Spotted Towhees occur from early October through mid-May.

Eastern Towhee *Pipilo erythrophthalmus*
The Eastern Towhee is a fairly common winter resident in brushy fields, second growth habitat, and open woodlands, probably from early October though mid-May. Until recently, this and the preceding species were considered races of the "Rufous-sided Towhee." As a result, observers paid little attention to them, so little information is available about the timing and distribution of migrants and residents in Northeast Texas. It appears that this species is distributed fairly evenly across the area, though it may be somewhat more common in the east. There are a few published reports in the literature of possible nesting birds from the extreme eastern sections of the region.

Cassin's Sparrow *Aimophila cassinii*
The Cassin's Sparrow is a very rare migrant in Northeast Texas. There are three records: one was photographed north of Cooper, in Delta County, on May 10, 2000, followed by singles near Cooper Lake on August 25, 2000, and at Lake Tawakoni, in Rains County, September 18, 2000.

Bachman's Sparrow *Aimophila aestivalis*
The Bachman's Sparrow is a locally uncommon to rare resident in open pine woodlands in extreme eastern Northeast Texas.

American Tree Sparrow *Spizella arborea*
The American Tree Sparrow is a very rare winter visitor. Most of the few published reports from Northeast Texas have been in December or January, probably when colder weather from the north drives the birds into the region.

Chipping Sparrow *Spizella passerina*
Chipping Sparrows are fairly common migrants and winter residents throughout Northeast Texas. They breed in mature pine or pine-oak woodlands in the eastern half of the region. Elsewhere, fall migrants begin arriving in early October and remain through late May.

Clay-colored Sparrow *Spizella pallida*
The Clay-colored Sparrow is an uncommon to rare migrant, particularly in western Northeast Texas. It is rare and irregular in the east. Spring migrants are found from early April through mid-May and again in fall from September through early November. During migration these sparrows occur in a variety of brushy or open habitats from residential yards to open woodland and fencerows. In spring they are frequently detected by their distinctive buzzy song.

Field Sparrow *Spizella pusilla*
The Field Sparrow is a locally common summer breeding resident in early successional habitats, such as old fields, clear-cuts, and pine plantations, primarily in the eastern half of the region. It is very

rare and local in similar habitats on the Blackland Prairie. In winter these sparrows are common residents and occur in a variety of brushy and scrubby areas throughout the region. There is an influx of wintering birds into the region in late October or early November. These remain until about mid-April or a little later.

Vesper Sparrow *Pooecetes gramineus*

The Vesper Sparrow is a fairly common migrant and an uncommon winter resident in short grass pastures and brushy fencerows. The first fall migrants appear in October, often in the middle of the month, and become more common later in that month. They remain until April or early May.

Lark Sparrow *Chondestes grammacus*

The Lark Sparrow is a fairly common to uncommon migrant and summer resident—particularly in the Blackland Prairie and Post Oak Savannah—and a rare and irregular winter resident or visitor. Although a few can often be found during the winter months, a wave of spring migrants appears in early April. They nest around houses and barns, in gardens and orchards, and along fences, particularly in open areas. Breeding birds are largely gone by mid- or late October.

Savannah Sparrow *Passerculus sandwichensis*

The Savannah Sparrow is a common winter resident in a variety of habitats, including weedy fields and open grassland, and an accidental summer visitor. It occurs from late September through late May. One was noted in a bluestem field at Cooper Lake on July 29, 1994.

Grasshopper Sparrow *Ammodramus savannarum*

The Grasshopper Sparrow is a locally uncommon to rare migrant in the western counties of the region and an uncommon, localized summer resident in hay meadows and lightly grazed cattle pastures in the northern half of the region. In winter it is probably a rare and very local resident in cattle pastures and bluestem fields. Although secretive, these sparrows are easily detected by their insectlike song—which is often delivered from a tall weed or fence post. During spring migration, which extends from early April through late May, they are sometimes fairly common in all types of grassy habitats. Just what happens after the breeding season is a mystery as the birds simply vanish, only to appear in small numbers in grassy fields in winter.

Henslow's Sparrow *Ammodramus henslowii*
Henslow's Sparrows are uncommon migrants and winter residents in bluestem fields in the eastern half of the region. They are very rare and irregular in similar habitats in the western counties. They occur from October through late April or early May.

Le Conte's Sparrow *Ammodramus leconteii*
The Le Conte's Sparrow is a fairly common winter resident in old fields and pastures throughout the region. The first fall migrants or winter residents appear in mid- to late October. They become much more common in November and remain fairly common until April. A few are still present in early May and on one occasion has lingered until the middle of that month.

Nelson's Sharp-tailed Sparrow *Ammodramus nelsoni*
The Nelson's Sharp-tailed Sparrow is a rare, but possibly regular, spring and fall migrant in Northeast Texas. There are five recent spring records for region, ranging from early through late May, as well as a couple of older questionable ones for March and April. There are six fall records, ranging from early to mid-November. This overlooked species typically occurs in a variety of wetland habitats, including cattail marshes, flooded grasses, sewer ponds, and lakeshores.

Fox Sparrow *Passerella iliaca*
Fox Sparrows are fairly common winter residents in brushy second growth and scrubby habitats. They occur generally from late October or early November through mid- or late March.

Song Sparrow *Melospiza melodia*
Song Sparrows are common winter residents in a variety of weedy, grassy, or brushy habitats. They arrive in late September and depart by March or early April.

Lincoln's Sparrow *Melospiza lincolnii*
The Lincoln's Sparrow is a common migrant and an uncommon to rare winter resident. Fall migration occasionally begins by late September, although most migrants are usually not seen until early October. These sparrows are low-density winter residents and can be difficult to locate at that season. Spring migration begins in April and continues through late May. During fall migration and winter, the birds occur in a variety of weedy and grassy habitats, especially where scattered brush and young trees are present. During spring migration, they are among the most common sparrows and are most conspicuous in open woodlands with a healthy growth of understory vegetation.

Swamp Sparrow *Melospiza georgiana*
The Swamp Sparrow is a common migrant and fairly common winter resident. The first fall migrants arrive in late September and early October and remain until early May. They occur in wet grassy fields, overgrown pastures, and brushy habitats as well as along lakeshores and in cattail marshes around farm ponds and lakes.

White-throated Sparrow *Zonotrichia albicollis*
The White-throated Sparrow is a common winter resident in a variety of woodland and brushy habitats throughout the region. It is accidental in midsummer, with two records from Van Zandt County in late June. Most migrants begin arriving in early to mid-October and remain until late April and early May. An early fall migrant at Cooper Lake on August 7, 1998 (a tan-phase individual) provides the earliest fall record for Texas.

Harris's Sparrow *Zonotrichia querula*

The Harris's Sparrow is a locally uncommon migrant and winter resident in brushy habitats on the Blackland Prairie. Elsewhere it is irregular and quite rare. The first fall migrants usually arrive in mid-November and the species has been recorded in spring until early May. A small peak in late April or early May of birds in alternate plumage is probably evidence of spring migration for birds that have wintered south of the area. In winter Harris's Sparrows are found in brushy fencerows and scrubby fields, usually where vines and tangles and tall weeds (such as ragweed) and grasses are present. They seem particularly fond of bois d'arc trees *(Maclura pomifera)* and are often found in thickets containing that species.

White-crowned Sparrow *Zonotrichia leucophrys*

The White-crowned Sparrow is a fairly common migrant and winter resident, at least locally, in a variety of brushy habitats—especially on the Blackland Prairie. Most are the nominate race *Z. l. leucophrys;* however, several "Gambel's" White-crowned Sparrows, *Z. l. gambelii,* have been documented from the western sections of the region in recent years. White-crowned Sparrows have arrived by late September, though mid-October is more common, and they remain until mid-May.

Dark-eyed Junco *Junco hyemalis*

The Dark-eyed Junco is a common winter resident throughout the region and occurs in a variety of habitats. The first fall migrants arrive in mid-October, and they are usually common until March, a few remaining until the middle of April.

McCown's Longspur *Calcarius mccownii*

The McCown's Longspur is a rare winter resident or visitor, mainly in the western counties of Northeast Texas, primarily among flocks of Lapland Longspurs. There are only a few records—although the species is probably more regular than the records indicate—ranging from late November through early February. A very early fall migrant was photographed at Cooper Lake on September 30, 2000.

Lapland Longspur *Calcarius lapponicus*
The Lapland Longspur is a locally common migrant winter resident in plowed or fallow fields and on exposed shorelines in the western sections of the region and is rare and irregular in the east. Lapland Longspurs begin arriving after the onset of really cold weather—sometimes in late October but more often in mid- to late November. They seem to be most common during the coldest part of winter, in December and January. After a brief winter warming trend, they seem to disappear, only to reappear when the weather gets cold again. During these cold periods, large flocks are seen rising and falling in unison over the bare earth. Once on the ground, they crouch like mice and forage almost imperceptibly. They are often mixed with flocks of Horned Larks, and close scrutiny may yield a McCown's Longspur in the flock.

Smith's Longspur *Calcarius pictus*
The Smith's Longspur is an uncommon migrant and winter resident in the Blackland Prairie and Post Oak Savannah, occuring locally in closely grazed cattle pastures with a healthy cover of three-awn grass (*Aristida* sp.). It is rare and very irregular in similar habitats in the eastern sections of the region. These longspurs are usually not far from water, especially farm ponds, and the fields they occupy often have numerous small rain pools or other ephemeral wetlands that are maintained by winter rains. This species is easily overlooked, as most, if not all, suitable habitat is on private property. Smith's Longspurs begin arriving in late November and are found until late February or early March.

Chestnut-collared Longspur *Calcarius ornatus*
The Chestnut-collared Longspur is a very rare or irregular winter visitor, occuring mostly in large flocks of Lapland Longspurs or in small numbers in short grass similar to or slightly higher than that used by Smith's Longspurs. There are few records for the region, ranging from late November through late April.

Snow Bunting *Plectrophenax nivalis*

The Snow Bunting is an accidental winter visitor. A first-winter male Snow Bunting was present at Lake Tawakoni, in Rains County, from December 26, 1999, through January 15, 2000 (TBRC 1999-116). Photographs of this bird were published in White (2001).

CARDINALS AND GROSBEAKS: FAMILY CARDINALIDAE

Northern Cardinal *Cardinalis cardinalis*

Northern Cardinals are widespread and common permanent residents in almost all areas of the region. They are generally absent from pure grasslands and open cropland. They are found around rural houses and barns, in brushy or weedy fields, and in overgrown fencerows as well as in a variety of brushy and wooded habitats. Small flocks often form during the winter months.

Rose-breasted Grosbeak *Pheuticus ludovicianus*

The Rose-breasted Grosbeak is an uncommon to rare spring migrant and a very rare fall migrant and accidental summer visitor. Spring migrants are more common in the east, though they occur throughout the region from mid-April through late May. A very early spring migrant was recorded in Rusk County on March 27, 2001, over three weeks earlier than usual. There is a single midsummer record for late June. There are a few fall records from early September through late October. The birds sometimes appear at feeders in North Texas during winter, though there are no records for Northeast Texas at that season.

Black-headed Grosbeak *Pheucticus melanocephalus*

The Black-headed Grosbeak is a rare migrant and very rare and irregular winter visitor. There are about eight regional records, ranging from early October through late February, with an unusual record from the Longview area on April 27, 1996. This grosbeak seems to be most likely to occur during the winter months in the Pineywoods.

Blue Grosbeak *Guiraca caerula*

The Blue Grosbeak is a fairly common migrant and an uncommon summer resident in overgrown fields, clear-cuts, and similar areas with scattered trees or dense brush. The species occur between early April and late October or early November.

Lazuli Bunting *Passerina amoena*

The Lazuli Bunting is a rare spring migrant in the Blackland Prairie and Post Oak Savannah. It appears that small numbers of Lazuli Buntings migrate northward each spring through Texas' Blackland Prairie, with a few reaching the western portions of Northeast Texas between late April and mid-May. This bunting is very rare in the Pineywoods, though there is a record from Atlanta, in Cass County, on April 26–28, 2001. There are no fall records; the difficulty of separating this species from basic plumage Indigo Buntings may be a factor.

Indigo Bunting *Passerina cyanea*

The Indigo Bunting is a fairly common summer resident in moist second growth woodlands and brushy fields—often near water. The first spring migrants are found in early or mid-April, the species not becoming common until later in the month and into May. Fall migration begins in early August and continues until October, but it appears that most birds have gone by early or mid-September. Only a few stragglers are seen in October.

Painted Bunting *Passerina ciris*

The Painted Bunting is a fairly common migrant and summer resident in brushy fields and second growth woodlands, often in drier habitat than the closely related Indigo Bunting. A few arrive by early April, though most do not arrive until the latter part of the month. The males become territorial almost at once. Males stop singing and disappear abruptly in early August, while females and immature birds are seen until mid-September.

Dickcissel *Spiza americana*

Dickcissels are abundant migrants and fairly common summer breeding residents, particularly in the Blackland Prairie. They occur primarily as migrants in the eastern half of the region and are very rare in winter. The first spring migrants occur from mid-April to late May, peaking with the arrival of hundreds en masse in early May, when it is not uncommon to find several thousand individuals crowding into a grain field or a row of trees along a fence. The sound of their collective voices is almost overwhelming, and the sight is spectacular. During summer they are widespread in overgrown pastures, grasslands, and brushy fields with scattered scrubby vegetation. Some attempt to nest in grain fields, though many nests are destroyed by harvesting in early June. Fall migration is protracted, apparently beginning for some individuals in early August and continuing through October and possibly into November. Dickcissels are regularly heard calling early in the morning as they fly south. After late September they are seldom seen and are more often detected by their flight call—a distinctive *drrrrrt,* given in an explosive manner as they migrate overhead. There are a few records from feeders in urban area in midwinter, often with House Sparrows.

BLACKBIRDS: FAMILY ICTERIDAE

Bobolink *Dolichonyx oryzivorus*

The Bobolink is an uncommon but regular spring migrant in grasslands, agricultural regions, and cattail marshes—especially on the Blackland Prairie, though low numbers occur locally in similar habitats throughout the entire region. It is very rare in fall. Small numbers of males first arrive in late April. They do not peak until early May, often remaining for several days. Females seem to arrive a week or so later—sometimes after all the males have departed. The latest records involve females in late May. The largest numbers are usually found at Big Creek Lake in the cattail marsh and the surrounding grain fields, the Bobolinks typically associating with massive Dickcissel flocks. It is not uncommon to encounter small flocks, some numbering fifty birds or more (and a hundred or more on a few occasions). Bobolinks are sometimes found in tall weedy grasses and occasionally in closely grazed cattle pastures. There are a few fall records in the region between late August and early September.

Red-winged Blackbird *Agelaius phoeniceus*
Red-winged Blackbirds are locally uncommon summer residents and common to abundant migrants and winter residents. They breed in cattails and grassy fields near water. There are records for every month of the year, though they are more common from October through April or May.

Eastern Meadowlark *Sturnella magna*
The Eastern Meadowlark is an uncommon summer resident in old fields and lightly grazed cattle pastures and a fairly common migrant and winter resident in a variety of grassy habitats. It typically occurs in slightly taller grasses than do Western Meadowlarks. There is a noticeable influx of birds into the region in late September and early October. These remain until mid-April when all but the breeding population depart.

Western Meadowlark *Sturnella neglecta*
The Western Meadowlark is a locally common migrant and winter resident in agricultural areas on the Blackland Prairie—plowed fields, closely grazed cattle pastures, mowed fields, and roadsides with short grass. It is rare to uncommon in the Post Oak Savannah and the Pineywoods, occurring locally in short grass habitats. Although there is some overlap, Western Meadowlarks seem to prefer shorter grass than do Eastern Meadowlarks. The first fall migrants arrive in early October. By the middle of the month larger flocks begin arriving in suitable habitat. They are present in spring until March or early April, and there is one record for Big Creek Lake in late May.

Yellow-headed Blackbird *Xanthocephalus xanthocephalus*
The Yellow-headed Blackbird is an uncommon to rare migrant and a very rare winter visitor in Northeast Texas. It is most common in the western counties of the region, where small numbers

often occur with large blackbird flocks and frequently roost with them at night—particularly in cattail marshes. During the spring of 1998, unprecedented numbers of Yellow-headed Blackbirds were present throughout the area, with some flocks containing a hundred birds or more. Yellow-headed Blackbirds occasionally occur in large flocks of other blackbirds in winter as well. Spring migration begins in early April and continues through late May.

Rusty Blackbird *Euphagus carolinus*
The Rusty Blackbird is a locally common to uncommon migrant and winter resident. It occurs primarily from late October through late March, with individuals often joining roosting flocks of American Robins and Cedar Waxwings.

Brewer's Blackbird *Euphagus cyanocephalus*
The Brewer's Blackbird is an uncommon winter resident in cattle pastures, feedlots, and barnyards, particularly on the Blackland Prairie. This species apparently roosts at night in the tops of scattered trees in open grasslands and pastures, unlike many other blackbirds, which roost in cattail marshes, giant stands of *Arundo* reeds, or other dense vegetation. Brewer's Blackbirds arrive in October and remain until late March or early April.

Common Grackle *Quiscalus quiscula*
The Common Grackle is an uncommon summer resident and an abundant migrant and winter resident. By late July and August, flocks begin to form, some of which by winter will contain perhaps tens of thousands of birds. They are more solitary and less evident in summer, though they breed widely in weedy ditches and brushy habitats across the area.

Great-tailed Grackle *Quiscalus mexicanus*
The Great-tailed Grackle has become a locally uncommon resident in western Northeast Texas in the last fifty years, particularly in urban areas, around rural houses and barns, and in cattle pastures, farm ponds, and cattail marshes in the Blackland Prairie and

Post Oak Savannah. More recently these grackles have been found in similar environments in the Pineywoods in the extreme eastern counties of the region.

Brown-headed Cowbird *Molothrus ater*
The Brown-headed Cowbird is an uncommon summer resident, and an abundant migrant and winter resident. It is most common from August through May, when large flocks roam the region.

Orchard Oriole *Icterus spurius*
The Orchard Oriole is an uncommon migrant and a locally uncommon to rare summer resident. The species nests in open woodlands, often where cattle are present, around farmhouses, and along small creeks. The first fall migrants begin to appear by late July and are largely gone by September, though there are a few records for early October. Spring migrants and breeding birds arrive in early April.

Hooded Oriole *Icterus cucullatus*
The Hooded Oriole is an accidental spring visitor in Northeast Texas. The only record involves a bird described in a residential yard near Longview, in Gregg County, on May 14, 1995. Certain populations of this species are expanding rapidly in south-central Texas.

Baltimore Oriole *Icterus galbula*
The Baltimore Oriole is a fairly common migrant; a rare, localized breeding resident in summer; and an accidental winter visitor. Spring migration is from early April through late May, and fall migration is from early August through late October. The only winter record involves a male seen in Harrison County on January 14–28, 2001.

FINCHES: FAMILY FRINGILLIDAE

Purple Finch *Carpodacus purpureus*
The Purple Finch is a rare migrant and winter resident in Northeast Texas. It seems to have become much scarcer and less frequent

in recent years. The species occurs primarily from mid-November through early April.

House Finch *Carpodacus mexicanus*
The House Finch is now an uncommon to locally common migrant and winter resident and a locally rare to uncommon summer breeding resident in urban areas. The eastern population of House Finch has staged a well-documented invasion into the eastern region of Texas and is often found near populated areas. Some data suggest that House Finches are even displacing the obnoxious nonnative House Sparrow that occupies similar habitat.

Red Crossbill *Loxia curvirostra*
The Red Crossbill is a very rare fall migrant and winter visitor in Northeast Texas. The only records involve several that spent the winter of 1997–98 near Caddo Lake and four that were at Lake Tawakoni on September 7, 2001.

Pine Siskin *Carduelis pinus*
The Pine Siskin is an irruptive migrant and winter resident in Northeast Texas. It is fairly common in some years and rare to absent in others. The species occurs from early or mid-October through late May, principally at feeders, but also in weedy fields with flocks of American Goldfinches.

American Goldfinch *Carduelis tristis*
The American Goldfinch is a common migrant and winter resident. In summer it is a very rare and localized summer breeding resident in mature post oak woodlands along the Red River and at Cooper Lake. The first fall migrants occur in late August and early September, and the birds remain (often at feeders) until late May or early June. Oberholser (1974) indicated a breeding record near Paris in 1915. The only other breeding record was on July 30, 1994, when an adult male was seen accompanying a fledgling at Cooper Lake. There are additional recent summer records for Fannin and Lamar counties.

Evening Grosbeak *Coccothraustes vespertinus*
The Evening Grosbeak is a rare and very irregular winter visitor in Northeast Texas. There are only a handful of records, ranging from late November to early May—and an unusual record from Jefferson County on June 24–25, 2000.

WEAVER FINCHES: FAMILY PASSERIDAE

House Sparrow *Passer domesticus*
The House Sparrow is a common permanent resident in urban areas and around rural houses, feedlots, and barns.

Hypothetical Species

Brant *Branta bernicla*
A Brant that was seen at the Gambill Goose Refuge, near Paris, by numerous observers during its stay from January 9 to 25, 1969 was never documented. Although this record was accepted by Pulich (1988), it does not meet the criteria set by the TBRC for acceptance on the official list and is thus on the hypothetical list for Northeast Texas.

American Black Duck *Anas rubripes*
There are several undocumented records of the American Black Duck in Northeast Texas. Although some may be correct, the TBRC does not recognize the species in the region. Some of these reports may involve the similar Mottled Duck.

Whooping Crane *Grus americana*
There is a single sight record of a solitary bird from Smith County on April 16, 1994. Whooping Cranes normally migrate well to the west of the region, often in association with Sandhill Cranes. Although this one is possibly a valid sighting, there are no written details to support the record.

Wilson's Plover *Charadrius wilsonia*

There are three reports of this normally coastal species, all without details. O'Neal (1957) included two on her list of birds seen in the Commerce vicinity in the 1940s and 1950s, one on September 21, 1947, and another April 18, 1951. More recently one was reported on a small pond near Longview on January 1, 1994. There are no details for any of these sightings.

Yellow Rail *Coturnicops noveboracensis*

There are two undocumented records of the Yellow Rail in Northeast Texas, an old spring report from Hopkins County and a more recent one from the Grand Saline marsh, in Van Zandt County, on April 23, 1995.

Black Rail *Laterallus jamaicensis*

There is a single undocumented sight report from the Grand Saline marsh, in Van Zandt County, on April 28, 1995.

Northern Saw-whet Owl *Aegolius acadicus*

The only regional reports of the Northern Saw-whet Owl are both from the Caddo National Grasslands: an undocumented one on December 18, 1984, and one that was unaccepted by the TBRC on December 19, 1989 (TBRC 1991-6).

Northern Shrike *Lanius excubitor*

There are two old reports for the Commerce area of Hunt County, including a bird present from October 28 through November 11, 1961.

Plumbeous Vireo *Vireo plumbeus*

There is a recent sight record, with no details, of this western vireo in Longview on November 14, 1995.

Western Bluebird *Sialia mexicana*

There is an old sight report without details from Commerce, in Hunt County, in February, 1951; it is dismissed by Pulich (1988).

Bachman's Warbler *Vermivora bachmanii*
In *The Bird Life of Texas* Oberholser (1974) considered the Bachman's Warbler hypothetical in the state, citing a probably misidentified report of three birds near Texarkana from May 30 to June 21, 1971. There are no acceptable records for Texas of this species, which is probably extinct.

Connecticut Warbler *Oporornis agilis*
There are several undocumented or unaccepted reports of the Connecticut Warbler in Northeast Texas. Oberholser (1974) cited a fall report for Harrison County and spring and fall reports for Smith County, all without details. There are two additional unaccepted records, for October 2, 1991, in Longview (TBRC 1991-128) and April 26, 1994, in Jefferson (TBRC 1994-80).

Lark Bunting *Calamospiza melanocorys*
Oberholser (1974) cites a single winter record of Lark Bunting for Smith County, without details.

Western Tanager *Piranga ludoviciana*
Oberholser (1974) includes fall and winter records for Hunt County. Many of these early Hunt County records were taken from a local checklist (O'Neal 1957) that is full of errors (see Pulich 1988).

Baird's Sparrow *Ammodramus bairdii*
There are several undocumented reports from the Commerce area of Hunt County in the early 1950s (O'Neal 1957).

Bullock's Oriole *Icterus bullockii*
The Bullock's Oriole is probably a very rare migrant, and an accidental winter visitor, though most of the recent sightings have been of immatures or females with white breasts—a feature no longer thought to be diagnostic of the species, as some Baltimore Orioles can appear similar. Oberholser (1974) gives a winter record without details for Smith County.

White-winged Crossbill *Loxia leucoptera*
There is one unaccepted record for the region from Kilgore, in Rusk County, on November 24, 1996 (TBRC 1996-190).

Common Redpoll *Carduelis flammea*
There is an unaccepted record of the Common Redpoll from Commerce, in Hunt County, from February 18 to 19, 1978. More recently, two birds matching the description of males were seen at a feeder in Atlanta, in Cass County, on January 8, 2001.

Extirpated Species

Greater Prairie-Chicken *Tympanuchus cupido*
According to Harry C. Oberholser (1974), the Greater Prairie Chicken once occurred in grasslands throughout Northeast Texas. Little is known of its distribution or when the birds were last seen. There are unpublished reports of prairie-chickens on the prairies of Franklin County in the late 1800s.

Scaled Quail *Callipepla squamata*
Scaled Quail once occurred in virgin tall grass prairie on the Blackland Prairie of Northeast Texas. Specimens exist for Fannin and Bowie counties along the Red River.

Eskimo Curlew *Numenius borealis*
The Eskimo Curlew was probably a fairly common or even abundant spring migrant in the grasslands of the Blackland Prairie, although there are few records. The only regional record that survives is from Red River County in 1894.

Passenger Pigeon *Ectopistes migratorius*
This extinct species once occurred in Northeast Texas as a common winter resident and migrant. The last regional record was in Van Zandt County in 1897 (Oberholser 1974).

Carolina Parakeet *Conuropsis carolinensis*
According to Oberholser in *The Bird Life of Texas* (1974), the Carolina Parakeet occurred in Northeast Texas in the counties along the Red River as recently as the 1880s and 1890s. He indicates that the last valid specimen for the state was taken near Texarkana in 1897. In a previously unpublished letter written in 1854 to his father in Kentucky, Thomas Howell, an early Texas pioneer who eventually settled in Greenville, had this to say about the birds that he observed northwest of Clarksville in Red River County: "Birds of all kinds are numerous. Paroquetes are very numerous; they are beautiful. We had a glorious little fish-fry on the first of May on Pine Creek, about six miles from here. We caught seventy odd perch and other little fish, and enjoyed ourselves a good deal in cleaning and cooking them. There were seven of us in all, no ladies of course, we stayed all day. The Paroquetes were making their harsh noises in the trees above us, occasionally we would scare wild turkey off her nest; sent the partridges helter skelter" (Howell 1854).

Red-cockaded Woodpecker *Picoides borealis*
The Red-cockaded Woodpecker was once more widespread in eastern Texas, occuring locally in pine forests in Northeast Texas.

Ivory-billed Woodpecker *Campephilus principalis*
The Ivory-billed Woodpecker once occurred in heavily forested eastern Texas but is now thought to be extinct in the United States. There are recent reports suggesting that the Cuban race may still persist in small numbers and persistent rumors of birds in Louisiana. According to Oberholser (1974), the last report from the region was near Marshall in 1918.

Introduced Species

Ring-necked Pheasant *Phasianus colchicus*
Ring-necked Pheasants have been released in several places over the years by private landowners in Texas. They have bred successfully for a while in some places, though there are probably no viable populations anywhere in the region.

BIBLIOGRAPHY

American Ornithologists' Union. 1998. *Check-list of North American Birds.* 7th edition. Washington, D.C.: American Ornithologists' Union.

Arnold, Keith A. 1987. *Atlasing Handbook: Texas Breeding Bird Atlas Project.* College Station: Texas A&M University.

Bedell, Paul A. 1996. Evidence of Dual Breeding Ranges for the Sedge Wren in the Central Great Plains. *Wilson Bulletin* 108:115–22.

Cahn, A. R. 1921. Summer Birds in the Vicinity of Lake Caddo, Harrison County, Texas. *Wilson Bulletin* 33:165–76.

Howell, Thomas. 1854. Letter to Dear Father, from Greenville. Copy in possession of the author.

Ingold, James L. 1995. *Checklist of the Birds of the Caddo Lake Watershed in Texas and Louisiana.* Bulletin of the Museum of Life Sciences 11. Shreveport: Department of Biological Sciences, Louisiana State University–Shreveport.

Kutac, Edward. 1998. *Birder's Guide to Texas.* Houston: Gulf Publishing Company.

Northeast Texas Field Ornithologists. 1993. *Birds of Northeast Texas: A Checklist.* Privately Printed: Northeast Texas Field Ornithologists.

Oberholser, Harry C. 1974. *The Bird Life of Texas.* Austin: University of Texas Press.

O'Neal, Nora S. 1957. A Checklist to the Birds of the Commerce Area, Hunt County, Texas. Photocopied.

Phillips, Allan R. 1986. *The Known Birds of North and Middle America.* Pt. 1. Denver: Allan R. Phillips.

Pulich, Warren. 1988. *The Birds of North Central Texas.* College Station: Texas A&M University Press.

Pyle, Peter. 1997. *Identification Guide to North American Birds.* Pt. 1. Bolinas, Calif.: Slate Creek Press.

Stutzenbaker, Charles D. 1988. *The Mottled Duck.* Austin: Texas Parks and Wildlife Department.

Tarter, Delbert Gordon. 1940. Check List of East Texas Birds. Privately copied. Copy in possession of the author.

Texas Bird Records Committee (TBRC). List of Review Species. *http://members.tripod.com/~tbrc/.*

Texas Ornithological Society. *Checklist of the Birds of Texas.* 1995. Austin: Capital Printing.

Wauer, Roland, and Mark Elwonger. 1998. *Birding Texas.* Helena, Mont.: Falcon Press.

White, Matt. 1998. *Birds of Cooper Lake State Park and Vicinity: A Field Checklist.* Natural Resource Program, Texas Parks and Wildlife Department.

———. 2000. Range Expansion of Fish Crow in Northeast Texas. *Bulletin of the Texas Ornithologicical Society* 33:6–9.

———. 2001. Texas Review Species: Snow Bunting. *Texas Birds* 3:18–21.

Wilson, Robert E. 1986. A Checklist of the Birds of Hunt County, Texas and the Adjacent Area. Photocopied.

INDEX

Accipiter cooperii, 45
gentilis, 45
striatus, 45
Actitis macularia, 54
Aechmophorus occidentalis, 29
Aegolius acadicus, 115
Agelaius phoeniceus, 110
Aimophila aestivalis, 101
cassinii, 101
Aix sponsa, 37
Ajaia ajaja, 35
Ammodramus bairdii, 116
henslowii, 103
leconteii, 103
nelsoni, 103
savannarum, 102
Anas acuta, 39
americana, 38
clypeata, 39
crecca, 39
cyanoptera, 39
discors, 38
fulvigula, 38
platyrhynchos, 38
rubripes, 114
strepera, 37
Anhinga anhinga, 31
Anhinga, 31
Ani, Groove-billed, 68
Anser albifrons, 36
Anthus rubescens, 91
spragueii, 91
Aquila chrysaetos, 48
Archilochus alexandri, 71
colubris, 71
Ardea alba, 32
herodias, 32
Arenaria interpres, 56
Asio flammeus, 70
otus, 69
Athene cunicularia, 69
Avocet, American, 53
Aythya affinis, 41
americana, 40
collaris, 40
marila, 40
valisineria, 40

Baeolophus bicolor, 84
Bartramia longicauda, 54
Bittern, American, 31
Least, 32
Blackbird, Brewer's, 111
Red-winged, 110
Rusty, 111
Yellow-headed, 110
Bluebird, Eastern, 88
Mountain, 88
Western, 115
Bobolink, 109
Bobwhite, Northern, 49
Bombycilla cedrorum, 91
garrulus, 91
Botaurus lentiginosus, 31

Brant, 114
Branta bernicla, 114
canadensis, 37
Bubo virginianus, 69
Bubulcus ibis, 33
Bucephala albeola, 42
clangula, 42
islandica, 42
Bufflehead, 42
Bunting, Indigo, 108
Lark, 116
Lazuli, 108
Painted, 108
Snow, 107
Buteo albicaudatus,
albonotatus, 46
jamaicensis, 47
lagopus, 47
lineatus, 45
platypterus, 45
regalis, 47
swainsoni, 46
Butorides virescens, 34

Calamospiza melanocorys, 116
Calcarius lapponicus, 106
mccownii, 105
ornatus, 106
pictus, 106
Calidris alba, 56
alpina, 57
bairdii, 57
canutus, 56
fuscicollis, 57
himantopus, 58
mauri, 56
melanotos, 57
minutilla, 56
pusilla, 56
Callipepla squamata, 117
Calypte anna, 71
Campephilus principalis, 118
Canvasback, 40
Caprimulgus carolinensis, 70
vociferus, 70
Caracara plancus, 48
Caracara, Crested, 48
Cardinal, Northern, 107
Cardinalis cardinalis, 107
Carduelis flammea, 117
pinus, 113
tristis, 113
Carpodacus mexicanus, 113
purpureus, 112
Catbird, Gray, 89
Cathartes aura, 36
Catharus fuscescens, 88
guttatus, 89
minimus, 88
ustulatus, 89
Catoptrophorus semipalmatus, 54
Certhia americana, 84
Ceryle alcyon, 72
Chaetura pelagica, 71
Charadrius alexandrinus, 51
melodus, 52
montanus, 52
semipalmatus, 52
vociferus, 52
wilsonia, 115
Chat, Yellow-breasted, 99
Chen caerulescens, 36
rossii, 37
Chickadee, Carolina, 83
Chlidonias niger, 66
Chondestes grammacus, 102
Chordeiles minor, 70
Chuck-will's-widow, 70
Circus cyaneus, 44
Cistothorus palustris, 87
platensis, 86
Clangula hyemalis, 42
Coccothraustes vespertinus, 114

Coccyzus americanus, 68
    erythropthalmus, 67
Colaptes auratus, 74
Colibri thalassinus, 71
Colinus virginianus, 49
Collared-Dove, Eurasian, 66
Columbia inca, 67
    livia, 66
Columbina passerina, 67
Contopus cooperi, 75
    virens, 75
Conuropsis carolinensis, 118
Coot, American, 51
Coragyps atratus, 35
Cormorant, Double-crested, 30
    Neotropic, 30
Corvus brachyrhynchos, 81
    ossifragus, 81
Coturnicops noveboracensis, 115
Cowbird, Brown-headed, 112
Crane, Sandhill, 51
    Whooping, 114
Creeper, Brown, 84
Crossbill, Red, 113
    White-winged, 117
Crotophaga sulcirostris, 68
Crow, American, 81
    Fish, 81
Cuckoo, Black-billed, 67
    Yellow-billed, 68
Curlew, Eskimo, 117
    Long-billed, 55
Cyanocitta cristata, 80
Cygnus columbianus, 37

Dendrocygna autumnalis, 36
    bicolor, 36
Dendroica caerulescens, 94
    castanea, 95
    cerulea, 96
    coronata, 94
    discolor, 95
    dominica, 94
    fusca, 94
    magnolia, 93
    palmarum, 95
    penslyvanica, 93
    petechia, 93
    pinus, 94
    striata, 95
    tigrina, 93
    virens, 94
Dickcissel, 109
Dolichonyx oryzivorus, 109
Dove, Inca, 67
    Mourning, 67
    Rock, 66
    White-winged, 67
Dowitcher, Long-billed, 58
    Short-billed, 58
Dryocopus pileatus, 74
Duck, American Black, 114
    Black-bellied Whistling, 36
    Fulvous Whistling, 36
    Harlequin, 41
    Long-tailed, 42
    Mottled, 38
    Ring-necked, 40
    Ruddy, 43
    Wood, 37
Dumatella carolinensis, 89
Dunlin, 57

Eagle, Bald, 44
    Golden, 48
Ectopistes migratorius, 117
Egret, Cattle 33
    Great, 32
    Reddish, 33
    Snowy, 32
Egretta caerula, 32
    rufescens, 33
    thula, 32
    tricolor, 33

Elanoides, forficatus, 44
Elanus leucurus, 44
Empidonax alnorum, 75
  flaviventris, 75
  minimus, 76
  traillii, 75
  virescens, 75
Eremophila alpestris, 81
Eudocimus albus, 34
Euphagus carolinus, 111
  cyanocephalus, 111

Falco columbarius, 48
  mexicanus, 49
  peregrinus, 49
  sparverius, 48
Falcon, Peregrine, 49
  Prairie, 49
Finch, House, 113
  Purple, 112
Flicker, Northern, 74
Flycatcher, "Traill's", 75
  Acadian, 75
  Alder, 75
  Ash-throated, 77
  Great Crested, 77
  Least, 76
  Olive-sided, 75
  Scissor-tailed, 78
  Vermilion, 77
  Willow, 75
  Yellow-bellied, 75
Fregata magnificens, 31
Frigatebird, Magnificent, 31
Fulica americana, 51

Gadwall, 37
Gallinago gallinago, 58
Gallinule, Purple, 50
Gallinus chloropus, 50
Geococcyx californicus, 68
Geothlypis trichas, 98
Gnatcatcher, Blue-gray, 87
Godwit, Hudsonian, 55
  Marbled, 55
Goldeneye, Barrow's, 42
  American, 113
  Common, 42
Goose, Canada, 37
  Greater White-fronted, 36
  Ross's, 37
  Snow, 36
Goshawk, Northern, 45
Grackle, Common, 111
  Great-tailed, 111
Grebe, Eared, 29
  Horned, 29
  Red-necked, 29
  Western, 29
Grosbeak, Black-headed, 107
  Blue, 108
  Evening, 114
  Rose-breasted, 107
Ground-Dove, Common, 67
Grus americana, 114
  canadensis, 51
Guiraca caerula, 108
Gull, Black-headed, 61
  Bonaparte's, 62
  California, 62
  Franklin's, 60
  Glaucous, 63
  Great Black-backed, 63
  Herring, 62
  Laughing, 60
  Lesser Black-backed, 63
  Little, 61
  Ring-billed, 62
  Sabine's, 63
  Thayer's, 63

Haliaeetus leucocephalus, 44
Harrier, Northern, 44

Hawk, Broad-winged, 45
Cooper's, 45
Ferruginous, 47
Red-shouldered, 45
Red-tailed, 47
Rough-legged, 47
Sharp-shinned, 45
Swainson's, 46
White-tailed, 46
Zone-tailed, 46
Helmitheros vermivorus, 96
Heron, Great Blue, 32
Green, 34
Little Blue, 32
Tricolored, 33
Himantopus mexicanus, 53
Hirundo rustica, 83
Histrionicus histrionicus, 41
Hummingbird, Allen's, 72
Anna's, 71
Black-chinned, 71
Broad-tailed, 72
Calliope, 72
Ruby-throated, 71
Rufous, 72
Hylocichla mustelina, 89

Ibis, Glossy, 34
White, 34
White-faced, 35
Icteria virens, 99
Icterus bullockii, 116
cucullatus, 112
galbula, 112
spurius, 112
Ictinia mississippiensis, 44
Ixobrychus exilis, 32

Jaeger, Long-tailed, 60
Parasitic, 60
Pomarine, 59
Jay, Blue, 80
Junco hyemalis, 105
Junco, Dark-eyed, 105

Kestrel, American, 48
Killdeer, 52
Kingbird, Eastern, 78
Western, 77
Kingfisher, Belted, 72
Kinglet, Golden-crowned, 87
Ruby-crowned, 87
Kite, Mississippi, 44
Swallow-tailed, 44
White-tailed, 44
Kittiwake, Black-legged, 64
Knot, Red, 56

Lanius excubitor, 115
ludovicianus, 78
Lark, Horned, 81
Larus argentatus, 62
atricilla, 60
californicus, 62
delawarensis, 62
dominicanus, 63
fuscus, 63
hyperboreus, 63
minutus, 61
philadelphia, 62
pipixcan, 60
ridibundus, 61
thayeri, 63
Laterallus jamaicensis, 115
Limnodromus griseus, 58
scolopaceus, 58
Limnothlypis swainsonii, 97
Limosa fedoa, 55
haemastica, 55
Longspur, Chestnut-sided, 106
Lapland, 106
McCown's, 105
Smith's, 106

Lophodytes cucullatus, 43
Loxia curvirostra, 113
    leucoptera, 117

Mallard, 38
Martin, Purple, 81
Meadowlark, Eastern, 110
    Western, 110
Melanerpes carolinus, 73
    erythrocephalus, 73
Melanitta fusca, 41
    nigra, 41
    perspicillata, 41
Meleagris gallopova, 49
Melospiza georgiana, 104
    lincolnii, 104
    melodia, 104
Merganser, Common, 43
    Hooded, 43
    Red-breasted, 43
Mergus merganser, 43
    serrator, 43
Merlin, 48
Mimus polyglottos, 90
Mniotilta varia, 96
Mockingbird, Northern, 90
Molothrus ater, 112
Moorhen, Common, 50
Myadestes townsendi, 88
Mycteria americana, 35
Myiarchus cinerascens, 77
    crinitus, 77

Nighthawk, Common, 70
Night-Heron, Black-crowned, 34
    Yellow-crowned, 34
Numenius americanus, 55
    borealis, 117
    phaeopus, 55
Nuthatch, Brown-headed, 84
    Red-breasted, 84
    White-breasted, 84
Nyctanassa violacea, 34
Nycticorax nycticorax, 34

Oporornis agilis, 116
    formosus, 98
    philapelphia, 98
Oreoscoptes montanus, 90
Oriole, Baltimore, 112
    Bullock's, 116
    Hooded, 112
    Orchard, 112
Osprey, 43
Otus asio, 68
Ovenbird, 97
Owl, Barn, 68
    Barred, 69
    Burrowing, 69
    Eastern Screech, 68
    Great Horned, 69
    Long-eared, 69
    Northern Saw-whet, 115
    Short-eared, 70
Oxyura jamaicensis, 43

Pandion haliaetus, 43
Parakeet, Carolina, 118
Parula americana, 92
Parula, Northern, 92
Passer domesticus, 114
Passerculus sandwichensis, 102
Passerella iliaca, 103
Passerina amoena, 108
    ciris, 108
    cyanea, 108
Pelican, American White, 30
    Brown, 30
Pelicanus erythrorhynchos, 30
    occidentalis, 30
Petrochelidon fulva, 83
    pyrrhonota, 83
Phalacrocorax auritus, 30
    brasilianus, 30

Phalarope, Red, 59
Red-necked, 59
Wilson's, 59
Phalaropus fulicaria, 59
lobatus, 59
tricolor, 59
Phasianus colchicus, 119
Pheasant, Ring-necked, 119
Pheuticus ludovicianus, 107
melanocephalus, 107
Phoebe, Black, 76
Eastern, 76
Say's, 76
Picoides borealis, 118
pubescens, 73
villosus, 74
Pigeon, Passenger, 117
Pintail, Northern, 39
Pipilo chlorurus, 100
erythrophthalmus, 100
maculatus, 100
Pipit, American, 91
Sprague's, 91
Piranga ludoviciana, 116
olivacea, 100
rubra, 99
Plectrophenax nivalis, 107
Plegadis chihi, 35
falcinellus, 34
Plover, American Golden, 51
Black-bellied, 51
Mountain, 52
Piping, 52
Semiplamated, 52
Snowy, 51
Wilson's, 115
Pluvialis dominica, 51
squatarola, 51
Podiceps auritus, 29
grisegena, 29
nigricollis, 29
Poecile carolinensis, 83
Polioptila caerulea, 87
Pooecetes gramineus, 102
Porphyrula martinica, 50
Porzana carolina, 50
Prairie-Chicken, Greater, 117
Progne subis, 81
Protonotaria citrea, 96
Pyrocephalus rubinus, 77

Quail, Scaled, 117
Quiscalus mexicanus, 111
quiscula, 111

Rail, Black, 115
King, 49
Virginia, 50
Yellow, 115
Rallus elegans, 49
limicola, 50
Recurvirostra americana, 53
Redhead, 40
Redpoll, Common, 117
Redstart, American, 96
Regulus calendula, 87
satrapa, 87
Riparia riparia, 82
Rissa tridactyla, 64
Roadrunner, Greater, 68
Robin, American, 89
Rynchops niger, 66

Salpinctes obsoletus, 85
Sanderling, 56
Sandpiper, Baird's, 57
Buff-breasted, 58
Least, 56
Pectoral, 57
Semipalmated, 56
Solitary, 54
Spotted, 54
Stilt, 58

Sandpiper (*cont.*)
Upland, 54
Western, 56
White-rumped, 57
Sapsucker, Yellow-bellied, 73
Sayornis nigricans, 76
phoebe, 76
saya, 76
Scaup, Greater, 40
Lesser, 41
Scolopax minor, 59
Scoter, Black, 41
Surf, 41
White-winged, 41
Seiurus aurocapillus, 97
motacilla, 98
noveboracensis, 97
Selasphorus platycercus, 72
rufus, 72
sasin, 72
Setophaga ruticilla, 96
Shoveler, Northern, 39
Shrike, Loggerhead, 78
Northern, 115
Sialia currucoides, 88
mexicana, 115
sialis, 88
Siskin, Pine, 113
Sitta canadensis, 84
carolinensis, 84
pusilla, 84
Skimmer, Black, 66
Snipe, Common, 58
Solitaire, Townsend's, 88
Sora, 50
Sparrow, American Tree, 101
Bachman's, 101
Baird's, 116
Cassin's, 101
Chipping, 101
Clay-colored, 101
Field, 101
Fox, 103
Grasshopper, 102
Harris's, 105
Henslow's, 103
House, 114
Lark, 102
Le Conte's, 103
Lincoln's, 104
Nelson's Sharp-tailed, 103
Savannah, 102
Song, 104
Swamp, 104
Vesper, 102
White-crowned, 105
White-throated, 104
Sphyrapicus varius, 73
Spiza americana, 109
Spizella arborea, 101
pallida, 101
passerina, 101
pusilla, 101
Spoonbill, Roseate, 35
Starling, European, 90
Stelgidopteryx serripennis, 82
Stellula calliope, 72
Stercorarius longicaudus, 60
parasiticus, 60
pomarinus, 59
Sterna antillarum, 65
caspia, 64
dougallii, 64
forsteri, 65
fuscata, 65
hirundo, 65
maxima, 64
Stilt, Black-necked, 53
Stork, Wood, 35
Streptopelia decaocto, 66
Strix varia, 69
Sturnella magna, 110
neglecta, 110
Sturnus vulgaris, 90

Swallow, Bank, 82
Barn, 83
Cave, 83
Cliff, 83
Northern Rough-winged, 82
Tree, 81
Swan, Tundra, 37
Swift, Chimney, 71

Tachycineta bicolor, 81
Tanager, Scarlet, 100
Summer, 99
Western, 116
Teal, Blue-winged, 38
Cinnamon, 39
Green-winged, 39
Tern, Black, 66
Caspian, 64
Common, 65
Forster's, 65
Least, 65
Roseate, 64
Royal, 64
Sooty, 65
Thrasher, Brown, 90
Curve-billed, 90
Sage, 90
Thrush, Gray-cheeked, 88
Hermit, 89
Swainson's, 89
Wood, 89
Thryomanes bewickii, 85
Thryothorus ludovicianus, 85
Titmouse, Tufted, 84
Towhee, Eastern, 100
Green-tailed, 100
Spotted, 100
Toxostoma curvirostre, 90
rufum, 90
Tringa flavipes, 53
melanoleuca, 53
solitaria, 54
Troglodytes aedon, 86
troglodytes, 86
Tryngites subruficollis, 58
Turdus migratorius, 89
Turkey, Wild, 49
Turnstone, Ruddy, 56
Tympanuchus cupido, 117
Tyrannus forficatus, 78
tyrannus, 78
verticalis, 77
Tyto alba, 68

Veery, 88
Vermivora bachmanii, 116
celata, 92
chrysoptera, 92
peregrina, 92
pinus, 91
ruficapilla, 92
Violet-ear, Green, 71
Vireo bellii, 79
flavifrons, 79
gilvus, 80
griseus, 79
olivaceus, 80
philadelphicus, 80
plumbeous, 115
solitarius, 79
Vireo, Bell's, 79
Blue-headed, 79
Philadelphia, 80
Plumbeous, 115
Red-eyed, 80
Warbling, 80
White-eyed, 79
Yellow-throated, 79
Vulture, Black, 35
Turkey, 36

Warbler, Bachman's, 116
Bay-breasted, 95
Black-and-white, 96

Warbler (*cont.*)
Blackburnian, 94
Blackpoll, 95
Black-throated Blue, 94
Black-throated Green, 94
Blue-winged, 91
Canada, 99
Cape May, 93
Cerulean, 96
Chestnut-sided, 93
Connecticut, 116
Golden-winged, 92
Hooded, 99
Kentucky, 98
Magnolia, 93
Mourning, 98
Nashville, 92
Orange-crowned, 92
Palm, 95
Pine, 94
Prairie, 95
Prothonotary, 96
Swainson's, 97
Tennessee, 92
Wilson's, 99
Worm-eating, 96
Yellow, 93
Yellow-rumped, 94
Yellow-throated, 94
Waterthrush, Louisiana, 98
Northern, 97
Waxwing, Bohemian, 91
Cedar, 91
Whimbrel, 55
Whip-poor-will, 70
Wigeon, American, 38
Willet, 54
Wilsonia canadensis, 99
citrina, 99
pusilla, 99
Woodcock, American, 59
Woodpecker, Downy, 73
Hairy, 74
Ivory-billed, 118
Pileated, 74
Red-bellied, 73
Red-cockaded, 118
Red-headed, 73
Wood-Pewee, Eastern, 75
Wren, Bewick's, 85
Carolina, 85
House, 86
Marsh, 87
Rock, 85
Sedge, 86
Winter, 86

Xanthocephalus xanthocephalus, 110
Xema sabini, 63

Yellowlegs, Greater, 53
Lesser, 53
Yellowthroat, Common, 98

Zenaida asiatica, 67
macroura, 67
Zonotrichia albicollis, 104
leucophrys, 105
querula, 105

ISBN 1-58544-193-7
90000
9 781585 441938